Canadian Art

by GRAHAM McINNES

TORONTO

THE MACMILLAN COMPANY OF CANADA LIMITED

1950

Printed in Canada

To my wife

Foreword

A GREAT DEAL has happened in the world during the past stormy decade; and much that has happened has been reflected in the smaller world of Canadian art. The fore-runner of this book,* written during 1937 and 1938, and published in 1939, has long been in need of extensive revision and expansion. This was necessary not only to take note of the developments of the past twelve years, but also to re-assess, in the light of later criticism, some of the conclusions then reached.

The present book, which has been extensively re-written, will, it is hoped, continue to supply the need for a brief critical work of reference, which, to judge by the steady sale of the earlier book over a period of twelve years, still exists. The new work attempts to be brief and general rather than detailed and diffuse. Our art includes not only painting, but sculpture and the allied arts; and these activities have been considered in relation both to each other and to the development of public opinion. The appendices contain information usually found in scattered form, and a select bibliography appears at the end of the book.

The enterprise of the publishers and the assistance given by galleries and periodicals has enabled the number of illustrations to be substantially increased. Through the courtesy of the King's Printer a group of colour plates has been included. Gaps necessarily remain, and the reader who wishes to fill them is referred to the appendix on art

* *A Short History of Canadian Art.*

collections in Canada. Here he will find works by most Canadian artists of importance, many of them available in reproduction.

My thanks and those of the publishers are due to the following sources for permission to reproduce certain paintings, and for the loan of plates and electrotypes: the Department of External Affairs; the Department of National Defence; the National Gallery of Canada; the Art Gallery of Toronto; the editors of *Canadian Art*; and various organizations and individuals whose names appear beneath the appropriate illustrations.

Grateful acknowledgement for advice in certain specialized fields is due to Dr. Marius Barbeau, H. S. M. Carver, Douglas Leechman, H. O. McCurry and Col. C. P. Stacey, O.B.E. John Gray and F. A. Upjohn of the Macmillan Company provided welcome guidance at the various stages of production.

It is a particular pleasure to record a debt to my old friend, Donald W. Buchanan, biographer of Morrice and co-editor of *Canadian Art,* who read the manuscript and made many helpful and constructive suggestions.

GRAHAM McINNES

Ottawa, September, 1950.

CONTENTS

ILLUSTRATIONS

(Between pages 80 and 81)

CANADIAN ART

CHAPTER I

The Background

G REAT ART IS UNIVERSAL", says Delacroix, "but it wears
the dress of its century." It also wears the dress of its
country. Whether that dress should be consciously created
and styled, with much pirouetting before the mirror of
public opinion, or whether it should be allowed to develop
of itself according to the changing whim of the designer,
are questions over which much ink has been spilled in the
archives of Canadian art criticism.

A national art is a delicately balanced organism. Too
much borrowing and it becomes flabby; too much aggressive
nationalism and it is swallowed up in the posturings of
propagandists and special pleaders. The best art represents
the reaction of sincere and sensitive people to their environment; and great artists will inevitably produce a great
national art in their search for full realization. But a
lasting and vital art demands more than the creations
of a few great men. It demands a general artistic awareness, an understanding of contemporary life, an intelligent
use of tradition, and the ability to see the universal in the
particular.

The history of art in Canada begins with the unquestion-
ing adaptation of the French settlers to the background
of the Lower St. Lawrence, and the rise and fall of a school
of architecture and woodcarving which produced some of
our most exquisite national heirlooms. It was followed by
a violent struggle to make art "Canadian to the backbone".
This struggle went on for many years. It was hampered
by the oppressive weight of misused traditions, the influence

of currently fashionable European styles and, occasionally, the hostility of Canadian officialdom.

Eventually, between 1912 and 1933 a national idiom emerged: significantly, in the period which began with the First World War and ended with the Statute of Westminster. Independence having been achieved, and loudly proclaimed, a period of self-examination followed, not unalloyed with doubt. A tendency arose to look inward and to desert, for a time, the bleak and brilliant realities of the Canadian landscape in favour of a more subtle and intimate approach. With the emergence of a new school in Montreal, and with the stimulus given to art and to the national consciousness by the Second World War, both points of view secured fresh and vigorous adherents.

In any estimate of Canadian art it has to be remembered that it is difficult for young countries to create an art of their own without some conscious effort. In Europe, artistic developments have been the result of slow organic growth. But such countries as Canada import wholesale the technical achievements and the artistic canons forged in foreign lands; and at first it is easier to use such tools to soften the impact of a new environment rather than to adapt them to its needs. In a new country, the impulse to imitate those whom we fondly conceive to be our betters is at first stronger than the impulse to create for ourselves in fresh surroundings.

A further complication was the rapid industrialization of Canada, which telescoped normal growth to an even more marked degree than was the case in the United States. The contradictions inherent in such rapid growth are naturally present in our art. But for this we may be thankful since, unless one is a genuine primitive, the production of works of art requires at least a comparatively stable material basis. The Indian could produce works of

2

art because his life was attuned to the tempo of the land about him; but the white man was grafting a highly complex civilization on to a land which, for some time to come, was alien to him.

The first pioneers are unlikely to be artists. A native idiom requires a people who have learned to think and feel in terms of their new home. Thus the establishment of a stable civilization on the banks of the St. Lawrence was essential to the creation of the art which reflected it. That this art failed to survive was due to the very rapidity of industrial development. The school of architecture and woodcarving was overlaid with British and American influences, and finally swamped by the machine, to which it was highly vulnerable, being an applied rather than a fine art.

With Confederation began the era of the larger Canada, and during the next thirty years some foundations were laid. The growth of material prosperity brought in its train the purchase of works of art by the wealthy, as a badge of social distinction. It also resulted in the formation of the Ontario Society of Artists (1872), the Royal Canadian Academy (1880) and the National Gallery of Canada (1880). In general, however, artists were as yet barely conscious of their surroundings, and the public was almost completely indifferent to artistic achievement.

During the two decades prior to the First World War, Morrice and Cullen began to explore the possibilities of the snowscape. Their new approach was fully developed by a body of younger artists centred in Toronto. Out of their efforts arose the Group of Seven (1920-1933) whose work gave landscape painting in particular and art in general a fresh inspiration and a new direction. By showing that Canada contained inexhaustible stores of subject matter, by applying the Impressionist palette to broad design and by painting from intimate contact with their surroundings, these men performed an invaluable service. Their influence is still felt in much of our contemporary painting and sculpture, and during the period from 1912 to 1930 they dominated the Canadian scene through sheer vigour.

The last twenty years have been marked by a reaction against the passionately native appeal of the Group of Seven, and a revolt against their sometimes harsh simplicity. This culminated in the more subtle and deliberately painter-like approach of a group in Montreal, largely French-speaking and deeply indebted to the School of Paris. They were concerned less with content than with style.

Finally, the years of the Second World War, with their buoyant effect on national pride and achievement, stimulated a vigorous artistic output, including the work of the official War Artists, and gave an enormous impetus to the appreciation of art by the general public. The fact that the last ten years have been among the most prolific in our art history may give social historians pause: but it is undeniable. Art flowed out of the studios and proliferated in film, in industrial design, and in all the various applied arts.

At the same time the public began to accord the artist his place as a producing member of the community, and national organizations and galleries arose or enlarged their facilities to meet a growing public demand. In 1949 the federal government recognized a duty towards a lusty foster-child by appointing a Royal Commission on National Development in the Arts, Letters and Sciences. This action might not move mountains; but it did mean that now official Canada was ready to admit that our art, like Alberta oil and Ungava iron ore, might be an exciting adventure, and perhaps an exportable national resource.

CHAPTER II

Native Arts

O F THE various Indian tribes scattered thinly over what is now Canada at the time of the coming of the Europeans, only the West Coast Indians of British Columbia can be said to have produced an art of high aesthetic worth. Elsewhere, pottery and other crafts have sometimes risen to the level of art, but on the West Coast, totemic art and handicrafts of a high order were produced. Though the presence of a mature and highly conventionalized art was recorded as far back as the latter part of the eighteenth century, no critical examination of it was made until anthropologists took the field. Their research, coupled with a growing interest in all primitive art, has mostly taken place over the last thirty years; and as recently as 1925 it was still fashionable to refer to the art of the West Coast Indians as "grotesque in design and crude in execution".

This art has had little direct influence on the main stream of our development, but it has often provided subject matter for painters who saw in it a certain affinity with their own work; and in the case of Emily Carr (1871-1945) it may be said to have provided an early and continuing inspiration. Until she turned, in late middle life, to the sombre naves and apses of the British Columbia rain forest, Miss Carr's work, both in subject matter and treatment, drew heavily on this totemic art; and throughout her life, as her books[1] bear witness, it exercised a deep influence upon her. Others who have sought inspiration

[1]Notably *Klee Wyck* and *Growing Pains*.

5

among the totem poles include such painters as Jackson, Holgate, Pepper and Pegi Nicol Macleod.

Though this Indian art is highly stylized and packed with social symbols, it has a definite kinship with its physical background. The West Coast abounds in lofty conifers; and these, together with bone, horn and argillite, provided the Indians with unlimited and easily accessible material. The lofty, intricately carved totem pole, preserving always its cylindrical mass, bears the same relation to the mountainous forest-clad landscape as one of MacDonald's rhythmic canvases bears to Algoma, or the low stone church of Quebec bears to the Laurentian hills.

Curiously enough the totem pole in its most striking form owes its development to the coming of the European. Using European tools, his art reached a size and perfection hitherto unknown, and as rapidly declined. Most poles were carved and erected during the past seventy to eighty years; and a heavy toll has been taken of them by the damp climate, which rots the wood very fast. But what remains is of great interest.

A complex set of heraldic family symbols, derived in general from animals, birds and fish, is conventionalized sometimes to the point of geometrical abstraction, and carved out of the cedar trunk in such a way as to remain true to the material from which it is hewn. It was only later that these strong plastic forms, created by the white man's tools, became degraded by the white man's paint. Before Indians learned to cover their forms with cheap house-paint, they created them from the wood itself, with economy of means and a high regard for the essential shape and quality of the tree.

The poles were erected in memory of the dead, and for ceremonial social occasions. They were not worshipped, but were held sacred because of their implications. But the elaborate heraldic design served the further purpose of demonstrating the owner's family tree. The pole was thus both a tombstone and a sign of the owner's claim to an established patrimony. It may be noted in passing that this particular form of art bears a superficial resemblance to that of the Maoris of New Zealand. Not only were the two arts comparatively recent, but the actual technique of erecting the poles (digging a shallow sloping trench into which the pole is slid and then slowly raised) is almost identical.

In other crafts, for decorative, domestic and ceremonial use, the West Coast Indians also excel. The skill of the woodcarver finds expression in the fashioning of ceremonial masks, many of an aloof and piercing beauty;[2] in the carving of wooden dishes, horn spoons and other domestic utensils. In all these the same unity of style is evident, for a conventionalized art is easily adapted to any particular material. The same elaborate stylization is also carried out in the ceremonial Chilkat blankets, woven of mountain goatswool and cedar bark, and in the baskets, woven from various fibres. Here it becomes completely abstract in design.

The Indians themselves have also provided subject matter for a large body of painting and sculpture. The bulk of Kane's work portrays their life and customs; Krieghoff made many studies of the Caughnawaga Indians near Montreal; Morris and later Henderson have painted the Indian; Hébert, Hahn and Suzor-Côté have carved him in wood and stone. There also appears to be one example of the direct influence of Canadian art on Indian design, though it rests largely on hypothesis.

It concerns the Eastern Algonkians whose chief artistic motif was a double curve adorned with realistic floral

[2] These masks, photographed in colour, formed the background to the film "The Loon's Necklace", which was judged "Film of the Year" in 1949 by the Committee on Canadian Film Awards.

patterns and geometric designs. Up until 1927 it was thought to be entirely a native figure. But Dr. Marius Barbeau has advanced the theory that its emergence was due to contact with early French settlers; and he takes their floral art to be derived from the rococo figures and ornaments of the period of Francis I. Dr. Barbeau cites the widespread influence of Mgr. Laval's Ecole des Arts et Métiers, established about 1675 at Cap Tourmente near Quebec; he also notes the predominance of these *motifs* in Algonkian art along the chief route of the fur trade during the seventeenth century. If this is true it is an interesting example of the inter-action of two cultures.

It will thus be seen that the art of the West Coast Indians is the only one to have influenced, even remotely, the broad stream of Canadian art. At the same time it is worth studying on its merits, and it may be noted that it has been thought essential to include examples of West Coast Indian work in most major international exhibitions of Canadian art. Moreover, native crafts, being in constant danger of extinction, are deserving of study by all whose view of art is not confined to museum walls.

No one can deny that the totems themselves are among the most powerful creations of this country. He who, wandering through the dense and sombre gloom of the forest floor on the coast of British Columbia, has suddenly come face to face with a staring totem, almost engulfed by spruce and hemlock, experiences a sensation of ageless and sinister power not unlike that conveyed by the great stone heads of Easter Island. These, he feels, were the work of the first Canadians; and he has an uneasy feeling that few among their successors have been able to produce, with such complete conviction, the spirit of the land which gave them birth.

CHAPTER III

Quebec: The Great Tradition —1760-1850

IN 1534 JACQUES CARTIER sailed up the Gulf of St. Lawrence, and planted a cross at Penouille on the Gaspé peninsula. But it was over seventy years before any attempt at settlement was made, and well over a century before immigration started on any scale. De Monts founded Port Royal in 1604; Champlain founded Quebec in 1608; but it was not until the latter half of the seventeenth century that the population of New France reached four figures. The history of French Canada is that of pioneers, and later small farmers, of hardy Norman stock, who slowly cleared homes along the banks of the St. Lawrence, and who sent certain of their sons far afield to explore, chart and develop the unknown hinterland. Their growth, up to the time of the Conquest (1759-1763), was slow, and they moulded themselves to the land which gave them their livelihood. In 1759 they numbered barely 70,000, immigration having ceased about 1680. Subsequently they increased enormously, there being now over 4,000,000 persons of French descent in Canada.

The history of their art is long and distinguished. First came the importation of late French Renaissance style; this was followed by a gradual adaptation and development after European influence had ceased to be important. Up to the time of the Conquest, we notice a colonial school of Northern French architecture, coupled with the development of a native school of woodcarving, which owed its origins largely to Mgr. Laval's foresight. From 1760 to about 1850 there occurred the growth, flowering and eventual

9

decay of a highly individual style in architecture, wood-carving and decoration, which, while it ceased to develop after that period, is discernible, as an influence, almost up to the present day. Louis Jobin, one of the last of the great woodcarvers, died as recently as 1928; and reminders of the great tradition still occur almost every time a new country church is consecrated.

When people migrate in a body to a foreign land, they take with them certain traditions in craftsmanship and design which have been handed down from previous generations. Thus at first the French Canadians built their churches and houses in the style peculiar to north-western France in the latter part of the seventeenth and the early eighteenth centuries. Constructed of wood—as was only natural in a country abounding with timber—most churches and many houses were subsequently built of stone to avoid the ravages of fire; and an architecture was produced in marked contrast to the wooden architecture of New England. The use of stone may also have been due to the masonry tradition in Brittany and Normandy. Laval himself was alive to the vulnerability of wooden buildings, and later on, bishops refused to consecrate churches that were not built of stone. The *fer blanc* roof also became an early feature of church architecture.

From the beginning, the French Canadians were a close-knit, homogeneous population, with a strongly paternalistic religion. So it is not surprising to find religious architecture predominating, and the enlisting of the crafts in the service of religion. The best art produced in Quebec was created for the church, and that art is not understood save in reference to the church which supported it and made it possible. In those early days, the church was a pioneer in secular and artistic as well as in religious matters. We owe it partly to Mgr. Laval, first Bishop of Quebec, that sure foundations were laid for advances in craftsmanship, and that the French Renaissance style was so firmly planted, whatever its later modifications.

Yet even before Laval's time, the Le Vasseurs (Levasseurs), expert woodcarvers from the valley of the lower Seine, had established in 1658 the Confrèrie de Madame Sainte-Anne; and the work of this group was an important factor in establishing a tradition of skilled craftsmanship in this and allied fields. The influence of the schools of handicrafts established by the Ursuline order was also widespread and profound, penetrating from Quebec to Louisiana, and fostering skills in statuary, gilding, leatherwork and embroidery which were passed on from generation to generation.

Laval established his Ecole des Arts et Métiers at Cap Tourmente, thirty miles down the river from Quebec City, about 1675. It reached its zenith in the years 1692-1703, but its influence was powerfully felt for long after Laval's death in 1708. The Bishop wished to make available for New France a band of highly qualified craftsmen, who could form a nucleus for future needs. To this end, he engaged from France sculptors, masons, coppersmiths, gunsmiths, builders, architects and woodcarvers, among whom were Gabriel Gosselin and Guillaume Jourdain, called Labrosse, who founded an illustrious family of craftsmen. Some of the results of their labours and those of their descendents can still be seen today, though fire, the Conquest, official neglect and "restoration" have taken a heavy toll. Owing to Laval's precautions, a fine standard of workmanship was established from the beginning, and when, after 1763, the local growth achieved originality and independence, it had a sure foundation of technical skill.

After Laval's death, the tradition of fine craftsmanship was carried on first by the carver Leblond de Latour, of

11

whom it is said: "Il fut un excellent sculpteur qui forma des élèves; ceux-ci partagèrent avec lui l'honneur du sacerdoce ainsi que l'art de manier le ciseau"; and later by divergent schools of carvers in Quebec City and Montreal. The Levasseurs of Quebec City—from Jean, who was born in Rouen in 1622 and came to Canada in 1645, down to François-Noël, who died in 1794—present an unbroken line of artistic achievement; and succeeding generations reflect the changing times. "Tandis que les premières recherchent le classique élégant et fleuri", writes Dr. Barbeau, "les deuxièmes introduisirent au pays le style à la mode de leur temps, avec des courbes délicates, des fioritures, de la rocaille et des 'crêtes-de-coq' ".

For the next fifty years up to the devastation of some of the churches by the English in 1759 ("Ruinée par les Anglais" is a familiar entry in parish registers) these craftsmen, with their own workshops, carried on the great French tradition. But after the Conquest, and for the next hundred years, an entirely original French-Canadian style of architecture and wood-carving developed. If it is possible to particularize, the classic exponents of the style were the Baillairgé family in Quebec City, a dynasty of carvers which worked almost continuously from 1741 to 1849. Near Montreal, Louis Quevillon, at the age of fifty, founded a firm with workshops at St. Vincent de Paul for the supply of church furniture and decorations to all districts. He had as associates Pepin, Rollin and Saint-James. Quevillon was more of a successful business organizer than an artist, but many apprentices were trained in his workshop, and graduated to work on their own account.

On the whole, however, a paternal, centralized and stratified society allowed little initiative, and hence there was little change. For two centuries, architecture and wood-carving developed in Quebec, but the growth was as slow as that of the people who were moulding themselves to the land. To realize the originality of the style they achieved, however, it is only necessary to see the actual churches and carvings. One of the interesting examples of the development of the style is the church of Ste. Famille on the Ile d'Orléans. Its history is in many ways typical of what happened to French-Canadian architecture with the passage of time.

The original church of Ste. Famille was begun in 1669 and consecrated in 1701, but in the early days a masonry tradition did not necessarily mean a supply of good masons; the building began to slip and had constantly to be repaired. The present church was built between 1742 and 1749, but today it represents a continual series of alterations and additions. The sacristy was added in 1750; in 1759 the church was badly knocked about by the English and the bell carried off. In 1763 a new bell was installed and new windows put in. In 1807 two side towers were added, and a centre tower in 1843. An upper gallery was added in 1853, and finally two side galleries in 1910, so that the church, as seen today, is the product of over two centuries of intermittent labour.

The church is also noted for its fine woodcarving. The five statues which once occupied niches in the façade of the church are of polychromed pine, six and a half feet high, executed with great dignity and feeling. They are the work of Jean-Baptiste Côté, of the school of Baillairgé, and are now in the Musée Provincial at Quebec City. The retable, which applies the technique of plasterwork to woodcarving, is a survival of the French School of the second half of the eighteenth century. It has been described by Dr. Barbeau as "untouched by those archaeological influences which were at this time (1820) transforming European architecture. It is not too much to say that

13

nowhere in the world was such work being done save in French Canada". The high altar, the work of the Levasseurs, dates from 1749, and in its vigorous handling of the contemporary French tradition is interesting as one of the last to show foreign influences. On the other hand, the sounding board, executed by Gosselin in 1795, already has the sturdy line which distinguishes it from the somewhat decadent *rocaille* work of the previous generation.

The church of Ste. Famille is a true work of art; but there are many others as fine. Perhaps the most important and beautiful are the Chapel of the Hôpital Général, and of the Ursuline Monastery in Quebec City, the church of St. Jean at Port-Joli, the church of Ste. Jeanne-de-Chantal, Ile Perrot, and the church of the Visitation at Sault-au-Recollet, near Montreal. This last is a noble building. Its period of construction ranged from 1696 to 1853, but even the Italianate façade added in 1852 does not seem to have impaired its essential unity. The sacristy doors (*c*1764) are panelled with carvings and scrolled in the Louis Quinze manner. Fleury David carved the ceiling and retable, both of which are extraordinarily fine. The church escaped "restoration", and in the opinion of Professor Traquair, is "one of the most distinguished monuments to the French-Canadian school in Quebec".

Domestic architecture does not, perhaps, present the same striking originality, but the style is distinctive. It is a long way from the enigmatic "Abitation de Québec" of Champlain, to the serviceable solidity and suave line of a house such as that at 92 Rue St. Pierre, Quebec City. Here again, there were two schools, those of Montreal and Quebec City; and in the course of time, the town house became the style for the country house in the outlying districts. Its most typical development was the so-called bellcast roof, which is still a feature of much Quebec architecture today, sometimes as a survival, more often in imitation of a tradition which has now outworn its practical usefulness. At its best, the Quebec house has style, simplicity and the charm of honest workmanship; though the charm has adorned so many Christmas cards and calendars as to have lost, to the casual observer, much of its first fine careless rapture.

More majestic in their dignity are certain public buildings of which one of the most important is the Hôpital Général at Quebec City, part of which dates from before 1670. It shows the vigorous tradition inspired by Laval and his followers; and though alterations have continued down to the present day, the central portion still remains much as it was in 1692.

There are other interesting features of Quebec architecture in its close identification, both in design and execution, with the woodcarving tradition. Though early buildings were of stone, the wooden house later imitated them, while the chimney was introduced as a mark of social distinction. The typical Quebec house is long, low and rectangular, without wings and with a steep-pitched hipped roof. In Montreal there developed solid, parapeted stone gables, resting on corbels and topped by a double chimney: one may compare this style with the elegance of the Château de Ramezay, built from 1704 onwards. But later, English and American influences were at work, and from about 1850 —perhaps earlier in Montreal—French-Canadian architecture ceased to develop much further.

The great tradition is today either imitated in the mass production of small houses, or else assimilated to the skyscraper in the edifice popularly known as the "railway hotel". The results of this latter venture are sometimes pleasant, and have given a superficial unity to railway architecture across Canada, the so-called "château" style often blending with steel-lined cement to present a well-integrated skyline and a strong mass. But while the average cottage and church in Quebec today stem, if remotely, from a sound parent tradition, the Gothic Revival and other eclectic influences have vulgarized metropolitan Quebec, especially Montreal; and so far, no native form has arisen to replace the old methods.

It is perhaps in woodcarving that the genius of the French-Canadian spirit was best expressed. The talent for exquisite craftsmanship and the sympathy for materials later spread to domestic furniture and utensils, rugs and baskets. These skills are being slowly dissipated as the more remote sections of the province are brought under the influence of the tourist; but the pride felt by French-speaking Canada in her traditions, and the work of such organizations as the Ecole du Meuble, are fighting a strong rearguard action against the extinction of a distinguished style.

The work of individual carvers, such as the Levasseurs, Gilles Bolvin, the Baillairgés, Quevillon, J-B Côté and others is often of great beauty and authority, with a strong rhythmic sense. In such a work as Côté's "Last Supper", carved in high relief as part of a retable, the intensity of the emotion is both sustained in and contained by every line which the chisel has incised.

Louis Jobin, who died in 1928 at the age of eighty-four, was one of the last descendants of the great tradition. He was apprenticed to Berlinguet of Quebec City, whose father had in turn been apprenticed to François Baillairgé. Dr. Barbeau, in company with the painters Jackson and Lismer, visited his studio before his death, collected information and made sketches of the carver at his work. In his tiny workshop at Ste. Anne de Beaupré, in an atmosphere "moyenâgeuse", he was still producing angels, saints and madonnas, carved with great strength and delicacy, with a northern Renaissance flow of angular but rhythmic line, and a true feeling for the essential mass of the wood. "Avec lui", writes Dr. Barbeau, "achevait de s'éteindre la Renaissance française". The surviving works of this fine school show the strength of a genuine tradition, the originality of a strong local growth, and a skill in craftsmanship which justifies the foresight of Laval.

Laval's successors were not always as liberal in the matter of art and handicrafts. In 1814, for example, Mgr. Plessis came to the conclusion that many churches contained "beaucoup de peintures détestables, dont quelques-unes étaient de véritables caricatures, plus propres à exciter la gaieté qu'à entretenir la piété des fidèles". He ordered the *curé* of Ste. Anne de Beaupré to cover statues of the four evangelists "avec des rideaux de serge ou de flanelle bleue ou verte, et de les tenir couverts." There is evidence that a wave of puritan feeling spread over the church in Quebec in the early years of the nineteenth century, and that many statues were removed and paintings altered to suit the newer ideas of modesty. But it may well be that as far as painting was concerned, Plessis was within his rights, for the earlier French-Canadian painters did not in general present their craftsmanship and creative ability to the best advantage in their painting; and their work is interesting chiefly from an historical standpoint. Père Hennepin, on December 6, 1678, saw and drew Niagara Falls. It is a naïve highly stylized record of a dramatic sight, but it is the first topographical drawing and the ancestor of the topographical school which flourished between 1775 and 1860. The Jesuit priests are known to have decorated early churches, but their works have been lost, partly through destruction by fire, and partly, no doubt, through the action of such prelates as Mgr. Plessis. There were, however, interesting personalities among them. One of them was undoubtedly the missionary Père Jean Perron.

17

When he found that his sermons were not receiving the attention they deserved, he painted pictures for his congregation, as an added attraction. La Mère Marie de l'Incarnation, herself an artist of some merit, who died in 1672, tells us of Père Perron's pictures. In one, "l'enfer est représenté tout rempli de démons si terribles qu'on ne peut les voir sans frémir". In another was shown paradise "où les anges sont représentés qui emportent dans le ciel les âmes de ceux qui meurent après avoir reçu le saint baptême". As a result of this, we are told, the Indians "écoutent le Père avec une avidité admirable". Père Perron appears to have flourished about 1670. Others tried to imitate his methods, "mais tous ne sont pas peintres comme lui".

But productions such as these are of documentary rather than artistic interest. The same is true of the work of Frère Luc, who about 1670-1680 made many pictures for churches in New France, including an Assumption for l'Eglise des Jésuites and an Ecce Homo for the Hôtel-Dieu at Quebec City. "On a dit du Frère Luc que son coloris était mauvais, sa composition médiocre, et son dessin excellent." One might have a worse epitaph than that. Not so fortunate was another Brother, Hugues Pommier, who came from Vendôme to New France in 1664. "Il faisait beaucoup de tableaux, mais personne ne les goûtait", and he returned to seek appreciation in his native land.

The first native Canadian painter was the Abbé Jean-Antoine Aide-Créquy, who was born at Quebec in 1749; but the woodcarving tradition seems to have occupied the creative energy of the French, and in general, it was not until the end of the nineteenth century that painters of worth appeared.

Exceptions, however, must be made in the case of François Malepart de Beaucourt and Antoine Plamondon. De

Beaucourt (1740-1794), working in the rich golden tradition of eighteenth-century aristocratic portraiture, produced some fine studies of local dignitaries; while Plamondon (1804-1895) painted, during the course of his long life, portraits of a limpid clarity and serenity.

In everything which called for skill and craft, the French Canadians excelled. There are decorative hooked rugs, carved wooden toys, iron, brass and metal work. The rivalry of two great silversmiths, Ranvoyzé (*c*1739-1819) and Amiot (*c*1762-1839) is still recalled in their chalices, pots, dishes, incense containers and the like; and in the St. Roch and St. Sauveur districts of Quebec City an occasional silversmith of distinction was still at work in the closing years of last century. There are the fine books of such men as Lemieux and Lafrance, and the pottery of Cap-Rouge. Whether it was dyeing, weaving, rug-making, the fashioning of furniture or basketry, the covering of church spires, the spinning and weaving of the *étoffe du pays* and the elaborate and beautiful *ceintures fléchées,* French-Canadian craftsmen turned out work of high skill and sensibility.

But the machine and the tourist did their fell work. The habitant today naturally obtains his domestic utensils at the local store; and though his life is much more self-sufficent than that of his English-speaking neighbour, he generally makes handicrafts for the tourist, often in the same bad taste, but rarely with the same contempt, with which the Chinese made chinoiseries for the European market. But a great handicraft tradition dies hard; nor is there any reason why the machine-made product should not exhibit good taste, provided manufacturers are willing to experiment. Meanwhile the French-Canadian tradition has left us with a vivid and vigorous school of woodcarving, decoration, crafts and architecture; and in the hands of

19

the younger painters and craftsmen of Quebec its vitality has been adapted to new forms.[1]

In the surviving remnants of this great culture—buildings with a sturdy originality and beautiful proportions; carvings austere and delicate, simple and strongly rhythmical; handicrafts with evidence of exquisite skill—lies the essence of French-speaking Canada. Here are shown certain basic and enduring qualities: painstaking and loving craftsmanship; manual skill of a very high order; simplicity of outlook; sturdiness of approach; and an integrity that is the result of an honest life lived close to the soil, a native sensibility and a respect for tradition. Perhaps the words of the voice in *Maria Chapdelaine* may pay a fitting tribute; "S'il est vrai que nous n'ayons guère appris, assurément nous n'avons rien oublié . . . Ces gens sont d'une race qui ne sait pas mourir."

[1]See Chapter IX.

CHAPTER IV *The Topographers — 1775-1860*

THOUGH THE TOPOGRAPHERS have no place in the main stream of Canadian art, both their widespread activities and the sheer size of their output claim attention. While art in Lower Canada was reaching a rich fruition, Upper Canada was artistically barren. The topographers kept alive what few sparks there were among the English-speaking inhabitants of Canada. They had no effect on the growth of public interest: that was caused by quite different factors. Nor were they Canadians. They were almost all English naval and military officers, or gentlemen amateurs, resident in Canada as aides, surveyors and explorers. They were artists only by accident. Their main purpose was to render accurately the topographical aspect of the country, often for scientific or military purposes. Nevertheless, their work is of great value, for they were active at a period when Canadian art, except in Lower Canada, was non-existent. Their task was often only the job in hand: the accurate recording of cantonments, the supplementing of surveys, the work of the interested ethnologist, or map maker, and the sketches of the amateur. They did not consciously strive to produce fine art, but they did produce works of merit, and kept interest alive, even though it was among a necessarily small group. During the period 1775-1840, theirs were the only paintings and drawings of any consequence. Krieghoff had only just arrived, Fowler was still in England, Kane had not

21

yet made his famous voyage to the West. But Krieghoff himself found the topographical influence strong in Quebec City, which suggests that it is not a force to be neglected.

The topographers may be divided into two classes: those whose approach is purely documentary, and those who infused a certain amount of creative imagination into their work. Père Hennepin was, as we have seen, the first topographer, though his simple enthusiasm puts him in a class by himself, for the true topographer was rarely naïve. By 1800, however, the two types were well in evidence. To the first belong Bennett, Duncan, Cockburn, Beaufoy, Davis, Coke Smyth and Downman. To the second belong Heriot, Bartlett, Short, Warre, Peachey and Eager. These men painted all over the country: Eager and Short in the Maritimes; Duncan, Peachey, Heriot and Beaufoy mainly in Lower Canada; Cockburn, Bennett and Davis mainly in Upper Canada; Bartlett throughout the East; Warre in the Northwest, on the Oregon Trail and on the Pacific Coast.

Père Hennepin (1640-1710) was the prototype of those brave Jesuit missionary-explorers, who did so much to chart this continent. He drew his famous view of Niagara in 1678, and about 1697 he gathered his experiences and reminiscences into a publication called *Nouvelle Découverte d'un Pais plus grand que l'Europe*. Later, many others visited the Falls—amateur, primitive and topographer— each leaving his record. Major W. J. Bennett (1787-1844) was one of these, and also worked round the Niagara Peninsula. His drawings were engraved by J. Hill and published by Megarey of New York. He is noted for an attention to elaborate detail, and the peopling of his landscapes with conventionalized figures.

Others who worked in Upper Canada were Captain Hancock, and Major Davis of the 52nd Light Infantry, who

did a series of six views of Niagara about 1818. Lt. James
Peachey lived in Canada for ten years prior to his death
in 1799. His best work was done near Quebec, and it is
in his drawings of the city, especially from Lévis, and in
views of the Lower St. Lawrence that his peculiarly personal style emerges. He had an imagination that continually strove to break through his passion for accuracy,
and thus elaborate detail is often curiously mingled with
attempts at formal design.

In Lower Canada, landscape material was perhaps more
fruitful. The Quebec countryside is more varied, and its
urban life was much more fully developed for the artist
who desired to make architectural studies. We may notice
James Duncan who died in 1881, having been made a
charter member of the Royal Canadian Academy. His
views of Montreal in the first half of the nineteenth century
are much prized by collectors. His pencil drawings are
weak, but he had a fine eye for architectural detail, and
a certain elusive charm. Another outstanding man was
George Heriot, whose prints, along with those of Lambert
and Bouchette, are a good guide to Quebec City at the
beginning of last century. He also painted along the Ottawa
River, and shows the influence of Claude to a marked
degree.

Captain B. F. Beaufoy, many of whose water-colours
were later lithographed, had a leaning to the picturesque
and sentimental. More famous, both as a topographer and
as a man, was Lt.-Col. J. P. Cockburn (1779-1847), who
also painted a good deal in Upper Canada, including the
by now almost obligatory Niagara Falls. He served in
Canada from 1823 to 1836, worked mainly in water-colour,
and published a series of lithographs of Canadian scenery.
He used a broad, open technique with light colours and
a wide sweep of line, and filled his landscapes with figures.

23

In the Maritimes the chief men were Mercer, Eager and Short. Col. A. C. Mercer (1783-1868) came to Canada in 1824, again in 1837, and took part in the settlement of the Maine Boundary Dispute. His views of Halifax and of Nova Scotia generally are light and bright, and executed with a pleasing freedom. William Eager (1796?-1839) who was also active in the United States, favoured microscopic detail in his landscapes, and thus missed, as did so many of the topographers, the essential majesty of the Canadian scene. Richard Short is perhaps the finest artist of the three. His views of Halifax, published in 1759, have yet to be equalled. He also published, in 1761, a series of twelve engravings of Quebec City and its environs. He had an excellent eye for the massing and grouping of buildings, a keen sense of perspective, and a manner of handling foliage which avoided the extravagances of Heriot. He was one of the few topographers to pay attention to sky, and obtained broad, sweeping effects.

The greatest of all the topographers was probably W. H. Bartlett (1809-1854). He came to Canada in 1836, painted at first round Halifax, and later throughout the eastern part of the continent, remaining on this side of the Atlantic for sixteen years. His two crowning achievements were the famous collections "American Scenery", 1840, and "Canadian Scenery", 1842. The latter has views in all parts of the Canadas, and is an important historical document. Bartlett used a free brush, and worked trees and buildings into his landscapes without overloading them; while his street scenes in Montreal and Quebec City are shrewdly observed.

Going farther afield into the land at that time in dispute between Great Britain and the United States, and the area between the Great Lakes and the Pacific Coast, we find one important personality. He traversed this country before

Kane, and his work, while slighter, and lacking Kane's immense documentary value, is of higher artistic merit. He was Captain Herbert Warre, who in 1845 went west on the survey of the forty-ninth parallel and made the trip along the Oregon Trail, as well as that from Fort Garry to Vancouver Island. Warre worked with Chinese white, wash and pencil line, on a heavy grey paper, which he used in free areas to great effect. With extreme economy of means he portrays scenes along the way. The mountains especially fired his imagination, and he makes of the Cascades something mysterious, diaphanous and aloof, like a Chinese painting. There is no sentimentalizing, nor an elaborate attempt at physical truth; the mountains are barely limned or suggested, with a few sure strokes. Warre is more than a topographer; he can claim to be the first Canadian painter of distinction. Many of his works were lithographed, but they lack the freshness of the originals, some of which can be seen in the Public Archives at Ottawa.

Two others were closely connected with the movement. The first is William S. Hunter Jr., who in 1855 published his "Ottawa Scenery", which was lithographed in Boston by J. H. Bufford. The drawings are not without interest, but it is as an early form of tourist literature that they mainly attract us. Hunter accompanied his enticing illustrations with patriotic and grandiose descriptions of the river, and a whole Baedeker of information.

Secondly, there is "A.K.", an artist working with the topographers and somewhat in their style. But he has a sense of humour and a tale to tell. He produced a series entitled "A picnic to Montmorenci", lithographed by Roberts and Rheinhold in Montreal, and published at Ottawa in 1868 by G. E. Desbarats. It shows, in brightly coloured, humorous drawings, a day in the life of a young Quebec gallant who takes his lady to Montmorenci Falls for a winter outing. After a series of ludicrous mishaps, the sleigh finally becomes stuck in a drift, is hauled out by a grinning habitant, and the party reaches home at a suspiciously late hour. The series shows a marked ability in caricature, and "A.K." is almost the equal of Krieghoff in portraying the comedy of manners.

The topographers worked mostly in wash and line, and their pictures were either lithographed or engraved, and then sold as a series or published in book form by Canadian and American firms. Some of the painters had their work printed by Currier and Ives. Occasionally the accompanying text is of more importance than the illustrations, as in *Recollections of Canada* by Lt. Carlyle, R.A. and Col. Martindale, which appeared serially in English magazines of the period 1759-1763. Until the advent of commercial photography, lithography and engraving were the main reproductive processes, and early artists, such as Kane and Krieghoff, used these methods widely. The originals are best seen in such collections as those at the Public Archives, Ottawa; the Provincial Archives, Halifax; the John Ross Robertson Collection of the Toronto Public Libraries; the J. Clarence Webster Collection, Saint John, N.B., and the Manoir Richelieu Collection of Canada Steamship Lines at Murray Bay, P.Q.

The topographical movement served a valuable purpose in keeping alive a transient interest in art. It died out when the country was better known, and when local painters began to arise, about the middle of last century. It was not a great art; but it has left behind interesting records, both historical and documentary.

CHAPTER V

The Pioneers—1840-1882

DURING THE PERIOD immediately following the American Revolution, the advent of the United Empire Loyalists profoundly affected the development of Ontario and New Brunswick, and had a marked influence in Nova Scotia, south-eastern Quebec, and indeed on all of older Canada. The Loyalists broke the virgin soil, gave the new land strength and largely endowed it with its present character and social customs.

An era of pioneer settlement was now in progress all over eastern Canada, and cities of a certain size had arisen. Within their limits there was a reasonably stable life; and as communities became better organized, they began to turn from a search for existence to a means of brightening it. In art, there was already the topographers' tradition. With the establishment of the University of Toronto and Queen's University, and with the educational work of Egerton Ryerson and Archdeacon Strachan, centres of learning arose. Indeed, it is to a private school, Upper Canada College, that we owe the formation of the first art society in Canada.

But conditions in Upper Canada were very different from those in Lower Canada. In place of a comparatively large homogeneous population with a common religion, there were at first only scattered groups in sparsely settled country. In addition, art in Europe had undergone, during the late eighteenth and early nineteenth centuries, a rapid change for the worse. Hence, there was no inspiring tradition to hand as in the case of French-speaking Canada. Fine houses were built, and their remnants may still be seen on the Upper St. Lawrence and in the Niagara Peninsula; there was also a record of manual skill in fashioning farm implements, vehicles and pioneer furniture. But there was no Cap Tourmente School and no professional outlook. Interest in art was kept alive by amateurs, and such painters as existed usually had to depend for a livelihood on painting houses, barns and signs.

The most active person in securing the interest of the layman in art was John G. Howard, drawing master at Upper Canada College. He came to Canada from England in 1832, and at once began to organize study groups. He had strong views on art, of a very conservative nature; and at his home, Colborne Lodge in High Park, which he bequeathed to the city of Toronto, he had a small private gallery. By 1834 he had founded the Society of Artists and Amateurs of Toronto, under the patronage of Sir John Colborne and Archdeacon Strachan. Its president was Captain Bonnycastle, a topographer of note; its secretary was Charles Daly. The society was not ashamed to nail its amateur colours to the mast. In the catalogue to its first exhibition there is a note to the effect that "members of the profession are distinguished by an asterisk"; and Daly, in a letter to Mrs. Howard, stated that "amateurs shall not be compelled to annex their names to their productions". The disguises "Amateur" and "A Lady" occur frequently in the list of exhibitors.

The only artist of note to send work was Paul Kane (1810-1871), then a young man who, a decade later, was to make his astonishing journey to the Pacific Coast. Kane exhibited nine paintings (including, as a matter of course, a view of Niagara). Many of the other works have titles typical of the attitude to art at this period. Included among many copies of old masters are such creations as "A

Dutch Toper", "Lioness with Whelps" and "An Idea in Perspective". Of the 196 exhibits, only twenty-eight are Canadian even in subject matter. Some ambitious designs for a guildhall, a theatre, and a new Government House provide a note of relief.

But having regard to the state of art in the community when it was founded, the society deserves great credit; it made a small beginning in a pioneering age. Howard gave the society his full support, but in such barren surroundings it is not surprising that it languished. People's minds were distracted from any interest in art by the Rebellions of 1837 and the general uncertainty which accompanied them. Howard, nothing daunted, started a new society, the Upper Canada Art Society, in 1841; but owing to lack of patronage this too was given up.

Only two exhibitions were held between 1834 and 1847, when Howard re-formed the original society. The letter accompanying the 1847 catalogue is an illuminating comment on the aims of the society, and the lack of support among its public. "It is wished to be observed", writes Howard, "that . . . the objects of the founders have been to give greater means and facilities for the study of the Fine Arts, being convinced how highly their cultivation will contribute to the reputation, character and dignity of the Province". Howard proposed to obtain, from Europe, "a collection of the finest casts of the finest remaining sculpture of antiquity, together with the choicest specimens of classical composition in foliage, with a series of other gems of antiquarian research".

We may notice the curious archaic bias to all this: there is no suggestion that members of the society might care to go out and paint the countryside about them. But Howard's intention at least was praiseworthy, for the object of these casts and specimens was "to promote the cultivation of pure taste in the various applications of design". Here, faint but clear, coming to us across a century of time, is the cry for the place of art in industry and commerce which, in our own day, has led to the foundation of the National Industrial Design Committee.[1]

"In order to the carrying out of this great object", Howard goes on, "the support of a generous public is indispensable . . . but I am satisfied from the general character and high discrimination of our worthy citizens that they will justly appreciate the motives that dictated the formulation of this society". This is laying it on with a trowel. High discrimination is a rare public virtue in any age; in the Upper Canada of 1847 it simply did not exist. As a natural result, the society, despite Howard's optimism, wilted and died; and as he himself sadly observed, it was so badly patronized that "my being treasurer, I had to pay £35 out of my own pocket". But this early failure, Howard's owlish solemnity, and the curiously stuffy methods whereby art was to be served, should not blind us to its importance. Later societies, while achieving more spectacular results, often lacked this spirit of altruism and independence.

Meanwhile, in the Maritimes, the arts burgeoned and as suddenly decayed. The great names here, until the revival of the local tradition during the past two decades, all belong to the first half of the nineteenth century. There are men such as William Valentine, a portraitist and miniaturist who introduced the daguerreotype to Canada; Robert Field, a master of engraving and oil painting; John Drake, an English portraitist, who was paid by a sitter in halfpence and had to bring a wheelbarrow to take the money home. At this time, too, art groups enjoyed a brief period of activity, and showings were held at Dalhousie College building in 1830 and again in 1848.

[1] See Chapter XIII.

But the period between Howard's venture and the year 1880 was one of expansion and material growth, and this had its effect upon artistic activities. Eastern Canada was becoming more prosperous, Confederation had arrived, and the project of a transcontinental railway was exciting men's minds. Several societies were formed which, if they had no immediate effect, were straws showing the direction of the prevailing wind.

From 1846, until its final establishment as the Canadian National Exhibition at Toronto, the Provincial Agricultural and Arts Association—a blessed union of seeming opposites —held displays throughout Ontario, at such points as Kingston, Ottawa, Toronto, Hamilton and London. There were art exhibitions at all these showings, as there have been ever since at the C.N.E.; but they were entirely subsidiary and handled in a most cavalier manner. The late Robert Gagen tells us of paintings stuck up like postage stamps, nailed to long slats across windows, walls and doors, and grouped according to subject. Meanwhile, the Art Association of Montreal had been founded in 1860; and in the previous year, Paul Kane had published his wonderful saga, *Wanderings of an Artist*.

In 1872 the Ontario Society of Artists was formed; it remains the oldest artists' society in Canada. By this time there were sufficient painters of talent to warrant the foundation of such a body; but the two greatest artists of the period, Paul Kane and Cornelius Krieghoff, died just before the Society received its charter. Both men are worth a searching glance.

Paul Kane was born in Ireland in 1810, but came to Toronto (York) as a boy of eight. He was fascinated by the life and customs of the Indians and, after travelling in the United States and Europe, he decided to "devote whatever talents and proficiency I possessed, to the painting of

31

a series of pictures illustrative of the North American Indians and Scenery". Between 1845 and 1848 he made two journeys which resulted in the publication of *Wanderings of an Artist,* and the execution of a large number of oils, most of which now hang in the Royal Ontario Museum in Toronto.

On his first journey, in 1845, Kane had the temerity to set out alone on his way to the Pacific Coast from Toronto. But by the time he had reached Sault Ste. Marie, wiser counsels prevailed, and he was persuaded to seek the help of the Hudson's Bay Company. Accordingly he secured the assistance of Sir George Simpson, Governor of the Company, and in 1846 went west with the Spring Brigade. They travelled by the Great Lakes and the immense portage system that leads through the Rainy River and the Lake of the Woods to Lake Winnipeg and Norway House. Thence they ascended the Saskatchewan by canoe and horse to Fort Edmonton, crossed the Rockies and descended the Columbia to Fort Vancouver in the present state of Washington. Kane returned by the same route, with side-excursions to the Grand Coulée and to the country of the Crees and Blackfeet. He arrived back in Toronto in October, 1848, after suffering incredible hardships and almost losing the use of his feet through an affliction known as *mal de racquet,* to which the inexpert snowshoer is particularly prone. During his travels he lived the life of the true *voyageur*; but he also found time to make over five hundred detailed sketches. His book was published in 1859, and in 1871 he died and is buried in St. James' churchyard in Toronto.

There is a variety of opinions as to the value of Kane's art. One critic has described his work as "merely of historical interest", and has suggested that while "Jacobi and Fowler strove to produce art, Krieghoff and Kane were

anecdotic". On the other hand, C. W. Jefferys observes
that Kane's pictures "possess considerable artistic merit,
and are extremely valuable as records of the vanished life
of the North West". Of course, Kane has his limitations.
He saw the prairies and the foothills through a European
haze; his Indians pose and posture after the manner of
David's mock-heroics; his horses are "the ideal Arab steeds
of the painters of the Romantic school".

All this is perfectly true; Kane is stilted in manner and
his colour is poor. But there is a vigour which comes inevitably from association with such subject matter; an
honesty and a simplicity that are both charming and disarming. Of the documentary value of his work there can
be no doubt. We should also remember that, even though
he painted in the European manner, he was at least painting his environment, which Howard and his friends, with
their casts from the antique and specimens of classical
foliage never did. Despite the often pedestrian quality of
his work, his spirit is that of a true artistic explorer.

There is little doubt, however, that his contemporary,
Cornelius Krieghoff (1812-1872), was the finer artist.
Krieghoff has sometimes been called the Breughel of Canada.
While such a label is altogether too generous, it is true
that as a sympathetic and humorous recorder of habitant
life he has had no equal. The son of a wallpaper manu-
facturer, he was born in Düsseldorf in 1812. After an
eventful youth, which included painting his way round
Europe, fighting in the Seminole Wars and working as an
artist for the United States War Department, he arrived
in Canada in the early forties. He lived at first in Montreal,
but finding a congenial companion in John S. Budden, who
combined the not always compatible virtues of the gay
blade and the art lover, he moved to Quebec City in
1853, where his best work was done.

33

He lived there, with one short interval, for over ten years, painting, holding auction sales, and becoming so popular amongst the garrison and townspeople that he was frequently reduced to copying his own paintings. His subject matter was the life of the habitant and the Indians, and a certain amount of the comedy of manners played in the social life of Quebec. Krieghoff gives a faithful account of the habitant's life: his habits, customs, foibles, how his houses looked, what clothes he wore and what sleighs he rode in. His sense of humour enables him to put wit as well as design into his compositions. His colour is bright, and though at times he descends to the level of caricature, his sense of composition keeps him from being grotesque. He is no mere anecdotal painter, and he clearly had a great zest for life. His canvases were painted during the period 1856-1860, and the best known are probably "Running the Tollgate" and "Chez Jolifou", which penetrate deep into the heart of the habitant's simple life, with its poverty and its humour, its piety and its dissipations. Krieghoff died in Chicago in 1872, the year the O.S.A. was founded; he is one of our first fine painters.

Apart from these two men, there was in the early seventies a group of painters in Ontario who raised the calling to the rank of a profession. Most of them were artists, with claims to competence based on grounds other than their ability to draw topographical landscapes or lionesses and whelps. The more important of them fall into two groups, the older men in their sixties—Fowler, Jacobi and Berthon; the younger men in their twenties and thirties —Fraser, Bell-Smith, Gagen, Martin, Verner and Cresswell. How these men organized themselves is told by Gagen. Up to that time, he writes, "Upper Canada produced no mature artist of note, save Kane. They painted Canadian subjects, but it was in the English manner". Now this was to change.

The driving force behind the formation of the O.S.A. was J. A. Fraser, an artist of considerable power, and a pioneer who later rendered the Rockies in a way that has yet to be equalled. He was associated with his father's firm of Notman and Fraser, and their art gallery was used for the society's first exhibition. On June 25, 1872, Fraser gathered some of these young men together at his home on Gould Street, Toronto, and the O.S.A. was conceived and founded on July 2. Fraser's peppery disposition, whatever troubles it aroused among his friends, was productive of nothing but good when there was work to be done. He stimulated enthusiasm and created unity.

The first exhibition was held in April, 1873, and Gagen gives a shrewd criticism of the work shown, pointing out that the achievement of the painters was still far short of their aim: the creation of a school of Canadian painting. He adds that it was the original intention of the founders that the O.S.A. should be a national organization, but that internal dissensions reduced it to the status of a provincial body. Of the third exhibition, Gagen remarks with commendable candour that it was "no improvement on the previous ones", and comments drily on the number of works that appeared with poetry attached. But the O.S.A. proved to be solidly based: the poetry disappeared from the frames and entered into the paintings.

In 1876, the society opened an art school, under the direction of T. M. Martin, and with a grant from the provincial government. In two years there were one hundred students registered, and after its due share of troubles the school eventually developed, in 1912, into the present Ontario College of Art, the society's connection with it having ended in 1884. There were already art schools with government grants at London, Hamilton, Kingston, Brockville and Ottawa.

While public interest was growing and art groups being established, artists were also active. Three older men, Jacobi, Berthon and Fowler, enjoyed considerable reputations which appear justified today only in the case of Berthon. Jacobi, in particular, has been consistently overrated. He painted in the brown, detailed style common at the time and had a passion for waterfalls; but he was a teacher of competence. Berthon was a portraitist with considerable claims to artistic merit, some of whose work can be seen at Osgoode Hall in Toronto, and whose study of "The Three Miss Robinsons" is a prim and engaging period piece. Daniel Fowler was a first-rate water-colourist, with a strong sense of line and a pleasant ruggedness of execution, noticeable even in his many flower pieces.

Among the younger men, F. M. Bell-Smith and Robert Gagen were starting on their long careers of service to art in the community. Both men were prominently identified, throughout their lives, with progressive art movements; and to Bell-Smith belongs the distinction of having painted the only picture of Toronto which makes it look like Paris. It is a study of the corner of King and Yonge Streets at the rush hour, and carries with it today an immense *fin-de siècle* nostalgia. Gagen and his followers were the forerunners of the Canadian Society of Painters in Water-Colour; and Gagen's meticulous marines still hold their freshness.

From the Maritimes came Robert Harris, a portraitist whose "Fathers of Confederation" is known to every schoolboy in Canada. The painting is illustration of the highest order, and it is safe to say that in so far as the founding Fathers have any reality for a younger generation, it is through Harris' carefully arranged group. A finer artist was William Cruickshank, with a tough, wiry quality in his drawing and a good sense of composition. On a lesser scale we may note William Cresswell, T. M. Martin and L. R. O'Brien, later president of the Academy. It was also at this time that Paul Peel, two-thirds of the way through his short life, was showing that flashy technical brilliance which has caused "After the Bath" to gain such an exaggerated reputation. More interesting from the standpoint of art and the public, was the rise of two fine cartoonists, J. W. Bengough and Henri Julien. Both were born in 1851, and at this time each was moving toward his mature style. They were to give Canada a reputation in the world of political cartooning which it was not to retrieve until the advent, in the 1940's, of Robert LaPalme.

Both Bengough and Julien contributed to *Grip,* a humorous magazine founded in 1873 and continuing for twenty years; and subsequently Bengough on the Toronto *Globe* and Julien on the *Montreal Daily Star* kept cartooning at a high level. Julien's famous "Bytown Coons" series, which pilloried Laurier's second ministry, and Bengough's satirical comments on the construction and financing of the C.P.R. are vivid relics of an age when comment was a good deal more outspoken than it is now.

At the close of this period came the foundation of the Royal Canadian Academy and the National Gallery of Canada. The establishment of these two bodies marks the close of the pioneering era in the development of art institutions. In 1878 the Marquis of Lorne became Governor-General, and both he and his wife, Princess Louise, showed a lively interest in art. The growth of material prosperity had given artists some degree of security and had interested wealthy people in acquiring works of art. A number of painters, led by O'Brien, asked the Governor-General for his support in placing official art on a firm base, and in

1879 were planned, as an indirect result of this approach, both the Academy and the National Gallery. They were founded in the same year, 1880, with basically the same idea behind them: "the encouragement of design as applied to painting, sculpture, architecture, engraving and the industrial arts, and the promotion and support of education leading to the production of beautiful and excellent work in manufactures".

But these things cannot be achieved by statute; and in practice all that happened was that while the National Gallery slowly began to build up a fine permanent collection and later encouraged art by means of extension activities, the Academy became the repository of official art, and at least one of its functions lapsed almost completely. This was the fostering of "designs and manufactures . . . and designs for all sorts of useful things, from wearing apparel and embroidery . . . to new stones and implements". Whose voice does one detect here? Was it that of the temporarily exiled English lady of gentle breeding and useful accomplishments? Or was it an echo of the teachings of Ruskin and William Morris? Whatever the voice, it had reckoned without the land of its adoption; and against the harsh realities of the Laurentian Shield, it withered and died. But in the growing cities an audience could be found; and thus it was that until recent years the Academy remained the official spokesman of the studio, with its varnishings, its hangings "on the line", and its dependence on social rather than on critical esteem.

No one questions the value of the conservative element in painting; but it is usually a mistake to give conservatism an official aura and to make it the layman's yardstick for measuring the value of art. Nothing was more praiseworthy in intent nor more deadly in result than the creation of an official art body at a time when serious painting in Canada had only just begun. The National Gallery also stagnated for nearly thirty years after its foundation. But while the Academy, by its very retreat into itself, tended to have less and less effect on the growth of art, the Gallery, in alliance with younger institutions, tended to assume some of the Academy's original functions. Thus the Marquis of Lorne's original purpose, was, after the lapse of a generation, on its way to achievement; and the necessary machinery and channels of communication had been set up for the use of creative national movements as they might arise.

Until 1884, the Gallery was merely a room in the old Supreme Court Building at Ottawa; and three years later, when it was moved to the Fisheries Building, it contained only 101 "works". It had no staff, no quarters and no policy. But the Academy went rapidly ahead. Lists of painters were prepared in Toronto and Montreal, and full-blown Academicians were created at one stroke, though many of them could by no conceivable stretch of the imagination be called artists. O'Brien became President, Napoléon Bourassa, Vice-President, and Marmaduke Matthews, Secretary. In March, 1880, the first exhibition was held. There was a good press, but some controversy over the wisdom of starting an academy so very early. In July, 1881, a constitution was adopted, and in May, 1882, the Royal Canadian Academy of the Arts Act was passed. Thereafter, exhibitions were held every year, at first in Ottawa, Montreal, Toronto, and once at Halifax. This last experiment was not repeated, owing to the lack of financial success. "We are frankly told", wrote a prominent Nova Scotia art lover, "that the Academy will not exhibit here because its members would be unable to sell their productions". For the last thirty-five years, all exhibitions save one have been held in Montreal and Toronto. The National Gallery,

39

however, sponsors an annual travelling exhibition, selected by the Academy, which is seen in all parts of Canada.

The first step toward putting the Gallery on a sound foundation was taken in 1907, with the appointment of an advisory arts council of laymen, the first members being Sir Edmund (then Mr. B. E.) Walker, Sir George Drummond and Senator Boyer. In 1913, under the National Gallery Act, a Board of Trustees was established. The Act stated that the Gallery had been founded with the object of the "encouragement of correct aesthetic taste [whatever that may be] and the Canadian public interest in the fine arts and the promotion of the interests generally of art in Canada". The government's grant was gradually increased as it became more aware of the Gallery's excellent programme of bringing art to outlying parts of Canada. The Board of Trustees became, in effect, governors of the Gallery and answerable for its policy to Parliament; though why they should have reported through the Minister of Public Works is one of those ineluctable mysteries of the official mind. It was also decided that Canadian works for the permanent collection were to be chosen "generally from all exhibitions of Canadian art" thereby avoiding the appearance of favouring any single group.

In 1910 Eric Brown was appointed the first full-time director. He held office for almost thirty years, and at the time of his death in 1939 had gained for the Gallery a reputation as an official champion of the national movement in Canadian art. Brown purchased major canvases of the Group of Seven as early as 1919 and also discovered the highly original talent of Emily Carr. During this period he also built up a carefully chosen permanent collection of European painting, to which the present director, Mr. H. O. McCurry, has added a number of distinguished works.

This examination of the development of both the Academy and the Gallery has carried us forward in time well beyond the pioneer period of art institutions. It is now necessary to retrace our steps, and examine what was going on in the minds and on the canvases of those whose works were later to fill them.

CHAPTER VI   *The Impact of Impressionism 1890-1920*

B<small>ETWEEN</small> 1890 <small>AND</small> 1920 the essential foundations of contemporary Canadian art were laid. It was an era of an awakening critical faculty; it saw advances in technical skill, in the artists' profession and in public interest. It was also the era of James Wilson Morrice, one of Canada's truly great painters; and it witnessed the impact of Impressionism on our palette. Impressionism not only produced fresh colour combinations undreamed of in earlier days; it also made possible a new interpretation of the Canadian landscape. The sense of exhilaration and discovery given by such methods led inevitably to an experimental approach. It was on this groundwork that young men, immediately before and during the period of the First World War began to build. Through their awareness they began to create an idiom more vivid and distinctive than any which had hitherto been seen in Canada.

But at first the tempo was slow. An interesting comment is to be found in a report made on the Canadian paintings which were sent by the Academy to the Colonial and Indian Exhibition held in London in 1886. The report was made by J. E. Hodgson, R.A., at the request of the Canadian Government. It shows us how Canadian art appeared to the eyes of a cultured European; and at the same time it reveals Hodgson's understanding of the peculiar position of art in a young country and the difficulties that beset its growth. This important document is worth careful examination.

Hodgson begins by quoting the critic of the *Magazine of Art* who had written that when you entered the Canadian section "you imagine yourself in a good European gallery much more easily than you can if you are in the fine art collection of any other colony". Commenting on this, Hodgson observes: "It has been rather a shock to me to observe evident traces of French influence—not the influence of the great French painters, but the rank and file of mediocrity . . . which is shutting out from us the clear bright air of heaven, and stifling us with the smoke and dust of studios".

He sees the difficulties Canadians have to face; they are "heirs to all the latest results of civilization, and yet they are in immediate contact with nature, still struggling to subdue her untamed forces". What Canada needs, he feels, is to turn her eyes upon herself. He applauds Fraser for going west in search of new subject matter, and closes with this rousing appeal: "The Canadians are beginning life afresh: I would that they could begin art afresh also. I should like to see Canadian art Canadian to the backbone . . . . a thing developed by nature in a special soil and climate". To be aggressively Canadian, is not, of course, enough; and to write off tradition as something moribund is thoroughly foolish. Tradition is dead only if we make it so, through too implicit a reliance on its virtues. It is the great touchstone to which experience must be referred, and all artists spring inevitably from it. But it can be adapted by those who are sensitive to a new environment, and that was what Hodgson urged. His clarion call, however, was not answered at once.

An exhibition was held, in 1881, in the galleries of the Art Association of Montreal; and a glance at the catalogue shows the sort of thing that is apt to happen when an interest in art is suddenly discovered by those to whom industrial development has given the means to gratify it. The exhibition is crammed with nineteenth-century Dutch painters, then regarded as "a good buy": such nonentities as Crabeels, Koekkoek, Grips and Tschaggeny. These strange creatures had as contemporaries Manet, Daumier and Degas; as compatriot, van Gogh. We also find "copies from the antique", and, in contemporary sculpture, a "Bust of Hebe" and "The Song of the Shirt". In fact, in many ways we seem scarcely to have advanced at all in the fifty years that separate Crabeels from "Lioness with Whelps".

A few years later, in 1893, another exhibition was held in Montreal by the Société des Arts. It was especially imported from Paris, where, however, it is doubtful if the painters were known outside a small circle of dealers. Certainly their names are now wrapped in decent oblivion, but it is worth rescuing them for a moment to mark the idiocy of some of the comments in the catalogue:

> HARO—Universellement connu.
> DELORME—Comme le fameux peintre, Henri Regnault, il peint de la main gauche.
> VAN DER ELLEN—Demeurant à Paris depuis un grand nombre d'années.
> ROCHEGROSSE—Comme dessinateur il peut avoir des rivaux, mais il n'a pas des supérieurs.

Such remarks tell us the direction, not of public taste, for there was none; but of those who aspired to guide it. They are cited in no carping spirit; equally foolish things are said today. But the basis of art has been broadened, and such exhibitions no longer form our principal fare.

The eighties and nineties, however, were strewn with mediocre painters, and with the distressing type of snobbery noted in the catalogue above. The only artists' society in existence was the O.S.A.; and even here the healthy materialism of the day, illumined by the dying gleams of Victorianism, made the ottoman and the whatnot the arbiters of taste. Robert Gagen assures us that the O.S.A.

galleries in Toronto were "the Mecca of the art of Ontario"; but one is tempted to doubt whether a place can properly be so described which enshrined the witticism: "I'm ailing; I'm not stout and may soon be on my bitter bier".

"We need a stronger national spirit . . . capable and generous criticism" wrote J. W. L. Forster in 1890; while J. G. Radford in the *Canadian Magazine* sounded the same note. "The greatest fact with many Canadians who have been fortunate enough to travel abroad", he writes, "is that on their return they advertise themselves as the pupils of some world-famed master. As if that would make any difference to their ability to paint". The fact that both these *cris du coeur* are still heard today does not rob them of their poignancy.

The work of George Reid (1860-1947) is perhaps typical of the taste of the period. His "Foreclosure of the Mortgage" proclaimed him the Fildes of Canadian painting, and there is no denying the continuing popularity of the picture as a genre piece. More interesting is Franklin Brownell (1856-1946) whose sparkling West Indian scenes have the brightness and hardness of diamonds. Other solid painters were Henry Sandham (1842-1910); C. M. Manly (1855-1924), with an interest in water-colour; and Robert Holmes (1861-1930) whose flower pieces have the glow of miniatures. Edmund Morris (1871-1913) painted among the Indians, and was able, from close understanding of their character, to arrive at an interpretation unequalled since the days of Kane. Florence Carlyle (1864-1923) is noteworthy as being one of the first painters who did not need to follow John Howard's advice and "affix the word 'Lady' " to her paintings. Prolific and vigorous at this time were F. McG. Knowles (1859-1932); Curtis Williamson (1867-1944), a portraitist of some power; and H. I. Neilson (1865-

1931) who is noted for the part he played in the development of Jean Bailleul's Ecole des Beaux Arts in Quebec.

More important is William Brymner (1855-1925) who was not only a liberal president of the Academy, but who, as director of the art school of the Art Association of Montreal, before the First World War, encouraged the younger artists and shielded them from irresponsible criticism. He instilled into his students precepts of hard work and sincerity, and though not a brilliant painter, he produced work of high competence, unmarred by mannerisms.

Two painters who gained more lasting reputations were Horatio Walker (1858-1938) and Homer Watson (1855-1936). Walker has been called the Canadian Millet with such frequency as to rob the phrase of its meaning. While his subject matter—a record of habitant life on and around the Ile d'Orléans—is akin to that of Millet, he is fundamentally an illustrator. He lacks Millet's psychological insight; but he may also be said to lack his sentimentality, and in such a painting as "Oxen Drinking" he attains a quite impressive stature.

Homer Watson repeated the lush rhythms of his native country in the valley of the Grand River in Western Ontario. He stems from the Barbizon School, but his intimate acquaintance with his subject matter, and a sturdy independence of outlook, coupled with a rich sense of paint, make his best work completely individual. The spirit of his canvases is essentially static, being a repetition, full of solidity and gentleness, of the same theme: the fecund beauty of nature. Watson was self-taught, and was far too prolific to attain a consistently high level of workmanship; but canvases such as "The Flood Gate" and "The Source" are minor masterpieces of dramatic composition, achieved through a natural feeling for paint.

By the turn of the century, the discoveries of the Impressionists had been brought back from Europe by students and young painters, and had begun to seep in from other sources. It was realized that the limited palette offered by the Dutch and Barbizon schools was capable of infinite expansion. New and brilliant colours were found, pearly with light, and Canadian painters were not slow to test them. The most successful experiments were carried out by Maurice Cullen (1866-1934) and M-A de F. Suzor-Côté (1869-1937).

Both these men discovered, through the new palette with its fresh colour and light, that the hitherto neglected snow-scape was capable of tremendous possibilities. Of the two, Cullen was possibly the finer artist; though in a different medium—bronze figurines of habitant life—Suzor-Côté revealed another side of his personality. Unfortunately Cullen, in middle life, became exclusively occupied in rendering light effects, and thus re-committed the error of the original Impressionists. But in discovering and exploring the snow-scape—through light leading to form, rather than through decoration—he performed an invaluable service. Greater than either of these two men, however, was James Wilson Morrice (1865-1924).

In the world of art Morrice is one of the most impressive figures this country has yet produced, and his influence on Canadian painting has been much under-rated, because he spent most of his life abroad. In point of fact, not only does a sizeable body of his work (twenty-six canvases and hundreds of sketches and drawings) show Canadian subject matter, but Morrice was a constant visitor to Canada long after he went to live in Paris. He gave up his visits only in 1914, partly because of the death of his parents, partly because he felt that his work was not appreciated in Canada, and partly because he had found that southern

climates brought fresh inspiration. "A painter should go
south, it cleans your palette for you", he is quoted as
saying. So he sought and found new subjects and new
inspiration in North Africa and the West Indies. Morrice
also exhibited frequently in Canada, and sent regularly to
the annual showings of the short-lived Canadian Art Club.

Like Cullen, Morrice adapted the Impressionist palette
to the Canadian scene: mostly winter studies in and around
Quebec City and Montreal, his birthplace. But he never
became tangled in the maze of light effects. He used colour
as a personal form of self-expression, in soft, free combinations, in flat areas of sensuous charm which melt into one
another, and express the reactions of a sensitive man to
the world without. Morrice was interested in atmosphere,
and the form which he created, while it is not often truly
plastic, is a combination of the decorative and the atmos-
pheric, and a peculiarly intimate beauty of colour. More
than any painter in Canada before him, Morrice used his
subject matter as a starting-point for excursions into the
realm of pure colour, closely and subtly allied in values,
which, unlike those of his followers, were not flat. All
his life, he worked toward the ease and freedom of his
final canvases. These sometimes show the art of a man
whose immediate intimate vision, while admirable for the
spontaneous sketch, failed when it came to organizing a
larger work. But these are only the defects of Morrice's
virtues.

The early influence of Whistler and Conder gave way
later to that of Matisse, with a resultant widening of his
colour range. Matisse speaks of the Canadian as "the artist
with the delicate eye, so pleasing with a touching tender-
ness in the rendering of landscapes of closely allied values".
It was this interesting experiment which led him away from
Impressionism to seek his own form in colour and pattern.

Morrice's biographer, D. W. Buchanan, has suggested that "Bonnard and Vuillard, leaders of a school which bears the inadequate label 'Intimist', are still closer to Morrice". If Intimists is a valid category, there is considerable truth in this. "Morrice was able", wrote a French critic in 1925, "with a deliberate tactfulness, to stop when everything had been said. His broad but concise technique, his oily and rich pigments did not resemble those of anyone else . . ."

Morrice was above all things a painter, and his simple, wandering life was dedicated with logical completeness to his art. Wherever he went, he took his own delicate, subtle, almost unchanging view of the world: a world seen through sensitive eyes, and re-arranged in terms of simple pattern and warm sensuous colour. "In his last canvases", writes Mr. Buchanan, "there emerges, as if it were spontaneously, a calligraphic design of broad strokes of pure colour. His sureness in values was, of course, the virtue that made Morrice so excellent a landscape painter. In the art of his last years, it seemed is if he had decided that if the values were true, the drawing could be left as free, as simple and as personal as possible". Contemplating Morrice's rich West Indian studies, his intimate glances at Paris, his strangely wistful Canadian landscapes, we would not wish it to be otherwise. It is a tribute to the firm hold which his work has on the Canadian public that his painting "The Ferry, Quebec", though distinctly personal and even esoteric in execution, should be almost as well known as "The Fathers of Confederation" or Tom Thomson's "Jackpine". Through his own particular alchemy, Morrice gave to this painting a quality which, apart entirely from the subject matter, is unmistakably Canadian.

During these years artists' societies had gradually begun to multiply. In 1905 the Canadian Society of Graphic Art was formed, and in 1907 the Canadian Art Club came into existence. But although ideas were astir, the public was still apathetic, and the older artists were curiously unaware of the new forces at work. For in 1907 a spirit of change was in the air. It cannot have been unconnected with the peopling of the West; with Laurier's resounding dictum about the twentieth century; and with the perhaps pardonable pride which expressed on a postage stamp, in doubtful grammar, the doubtful postulate: "We Hold a Vaster Empire Than Has Been". There was a growing dissatisfaction among artists with the stuffy prejudice against Canadian work, and the Club was founded to crystallize this resentment and to "produce something Canadian in spirit . . . strong, vital and living". The number of societies, clubs and organizations which have been dedicated to this purpose over the past fifty years is almost impossible to compute; but few of their activities can have been as strange as that of the Canadian Art Club.

Writing in *The Studio,* a Toronto lawyer and art lover declared that the Club had done much to foster sound artistic appreciation. While some years ago, he wrote, there had been little feeling for art among the public, yet now one could see "magnificent paintings by Israels, Mauve and Weissenbruch". That there should be paintings in people's homes is a fine thing; but that the Club should have taken pride in the importation of these mediocre Dutch canvases defies comment. In 1915 the Club was dissolved; artistically it had misfired, for it had sought to remedy a disease with palliatives. It remains an interesting example of the way in which the strength of a "rebel" movement can be dissipated through a misunderstanding of the causes of the malady it seeks to cure.

The Yearbook of the Arts, published in Toronto in 1913, gives an idea of the Club's contemporary background; and some of the criticisms are illuminating. R. F. Fleming,

writing of the Academy, heaves a sigh of relief at the fact
that "We have no Cézannes; all our art is sane, healthy,
worthy and inspiring". On the other hand, Wyly Grier,
later President of the Academy, states that, if the artist is
any good "he cannot paint acceptable Academy pictures";
and he scolds Walker for being too "European".

By 1912 the Ontario College of Art, the Royal Ontario
Museum and the Montreal Arts Club had been founded.
Professor Goldwin Smith had already bequeathed the man-
sion that was later to become the Art Gallery of Toronto.
The first "Little Picture" showing of the O.S.A. was held
in 1913. But the critics were still dour. "There is a great
deal of work exhibited every year which is merely ridic-
ulous", wrote W. B. Harte. "The generality of Canadian
painters barely escape being mere copyists and daubers . . .
perpetuating effects foreign to Canada". "Indifference and
lack of appreciation cause many of our best men to leave
us", wrote J. G. Radford in 1912. "Canada is either too
young, too poor, too ignorant or too busy making money
to take much interest in art". Artists were "so imbued with
the idea of rapidly accumulating wealth that their work
is advertised in the daily papers . . . . and sold over the
counter at so much each". But even granted that the artist
has to make a living, Radford does not spare his art.
"Rarely one sees good figure work . . . the appalling
monotony of our landscapes . . . innumerable volunteer
critics airing their knowledge".

Yet in the midst of Radford's jeremiad the way was being
prepared for the creation of a national idiom; and even
as he penned his lugubrious lines, the genius of Morrice was
in full flower.

CHAPTER VII

*A National Idiom Emerges
1912-1933*

IN 1910 THE ROYAL CANADIAN ACADEMY sent an exhibition
to England. The critic of the *Morning Post* declared of it
that "the observation of physical fact is strong, but the
more immutable essence of each scene is crushed out by
a foreign begotten technique". There was a group of young
men in Canada who were painfully aware of this fact.

Not all of them followed the same road, and three of them
—Milne, Lyman and Gagnon—were less concerned with
discoveries in subject matter than with discoveries in paint.
Clarence Gagnon (1881-1942) found his *métier* among the
villages of the Laurentians, and later illustrated a *de luxe*
edition of *Maria Chapdelaine* with exquisite monotypes.
John Lyman, a painter of great integrity, was to study and
paint abroad before finding himself as a leader of a
group in Montreal influenced by the School of Paris. David
Milne was already embarking on those wiry drawings and
spare dabs of paint which were to turn him into one of
our most interesting and personal landscape artists. We
shall meet Milne and Lyman later on; our concern at the
moment is with those who based their rebellion on a specific
and overt appeal to Canadianism.

These men loved the north country and believed that if
they sought inspiration beneath its clear skies and among
its bold patterns, a fresh approach would be possible. They
were drawn together through common aims, and finally,
in close association, they gave a new direction and a tremendous stimulus to Canadian art. These artists began to

work in the years immediately before the First World War. Some, like A. Y. Jackson, were already in the thick of the fight for progressive art in Montreal; others had found employment at the studios of Grip Ltd., a commercial art and engraving firm in Toronto. By the time war broke out they had worked in harmony together for some time; had made exploratory painting trips into northern Ontario; and had found there subject matter which moved them. They were conscious rebels, and the results, to their contemporaries, were startling. Here, for the first time, in a large, coherent and vocal body, were men deliberately setting out to paint Canada through Canadian eyes. Irrespective of the artistic value of their work, the discovery that it could be successfully undertaken, and the enthusiasm and controversy which it aroused, acted like a tonic on artists and gallery-goers whose palettes were jaded by paintings which one of them described as "drenched in brown gravy". Though Canadian art has matured greatly during the past forty years, it is doubtful whether any single movement in its history had such an immediate and far-reaching effect.

The eldest of the group was Tom Thomson (1877-1917) a farm boy from near Owen Sound, Ontario, whose passion was the north woods. Working at Grip Ltd. during the winter months as designer and letterer, he spent his summers in Algonquin Park as bushman and guide. Already he had begun sketching on small birch panels: attempting to distil, in one spontaneous painting, the feeling of his beloved north country. Of all the artists in the movement it was he who felt most strongly the appeal of the north, for he belonged to it.

Among his companions were Arthur Lismer and F. H. Varley, recently arrived from England, and both with strong memories of Yorkshire moors, rather than of the soft lush greenery of the home counties, so susceptible to

53

treatment along Barbizon lines. There was J. E. H. Mac-
Donald (1873-1932), a quiet, lyric spirit, whose superb
sense of decorative colour was later to get him into trouble
with the critics. There was Franklin Carmichael (1890-
1945), a young painter much interested in highly designed
water-colours. With F. H. Johnston (1888-1948), all these
men worked, at one time or another, at Grip Ltd., where
they secured the friendly interest of the writer and critic,
Albert H. Robson, always sympathetic to new ideas. They
sketched together and severally on Sundays, and began to
explore Algonquin Park, largely at the suggestion of an older
artist, J. W. Beatty (1869-1941), who had already seen
something of its possibilities.

On his return from Europe at this time, Lawren Harris,
a young painter of independent means and ripe for artistic
adventure, was introduced to these men by Dr. J. S.
MacCallum of Toronto, whose interest in their work was
already strong. Artist and doctor generously persuaded
MacDonald to give up his commercial work; later they
urged Jackson to come to Toronto; finally they erected in
that city, to their own specifications, the Studio Building,
where these artists were to create their new idiom. The
studios were completed in 1914, but the little group was
temporarily scattered by the First World War.

Late in 1913, however, Jackson had come to Toronto,
had met Thomson and gone painting with him; and through
close association the two men helped each other greatly.
Jackson admired the simplicity and quiet enthusiasm of
the older man; Thomson, self-taught, learned much from
the younger, fresh from the Académie Julian. From then
until his accidental death in 1917 at the age of barely
forty, Thomson developed fast. His sketches are gems of
pure colour, showing the instinctive reaction of a sensitive
man to a well-loved scene. They have immediacy, spon-

taneous freshness and clarity. They are painted with glowing sureness till, at the end, one vigorous sweep of the brush produces both colour and form. Thomson had a colour sense that lacked subtlety, but was admirably suited to convey the agate-like brilliance of the north country. In his canvases, his success was less certain, since the gap between the first vision and the final execution was necessarily wider.

Thomson evolved rapidly from the purely decorative and sombre to the dynamic and sparkling. But his sketches, despite their early technical fumblings, have that stamp of absolute conviction which makes his art so vital, so accessible and yet so very personal. He is a fine painter, but his importance lies as much in the inspiration he provided as in his actual work. His love for the north led his companions there; his early death, after he had been painting for scarcely four years, must have spurred them to greater efforts. Like Homer Watson, Thomson was an original; but because he painted in a more personal and distinctive manner, and because his subject matter was fresher, his work overshadows that of the older painter in the development of our art.

In later years there has grown up around the memory of Thomson a legend which makes the art historian examine his works more critically. The legend is that of the inarticulate artist-woodsman who dashed like a comet across the Canadian scene and died mysteriously at the height of his powers. It is a legend which has inspired both affection and reverence; but provided one realizes that it enshrines not only Thomson and his work, but his unrealized talents—his "might have been"—it is valid enough. Further, Thomson's work does bear out the legend. Though his canvases, with exceptions such as "Spring Ice", "The Drive" and "Pointers", are sometimes apt to be stilted, one is

tempted to doubt whether he would ever have improved on the limpid clarity of his sketches. Most of them are pure gems and bear the authoritative stamp of genius: immediacy, ordered beauty, and absolute certainty.

The contribution of his personality to Canadian art is nowhere better stated than on the cairn erected to his memory at Canoe Lake, Algonquin Park. The stones were dragged up the hill from the lake shore, single-handed, by Beatty; the inscription was written by MacDonald. One may be sure that to both artists these were indeed labours of pure love. The inscription reads thus:

> "To the memory of Tom Thomson, artist, woodsman and guide, who was drowned in Canoe Lake, July 8, 1917. He lived humbly but passionately with the wild. It made him brother to all untamed things in nature. It drew him apart and revealed itself wonderfully to him. It sent him out from the woods only to show these revelations through his art, and it took him to itself at last."

In 1916, MacDonald sent to the O.S.A. a painting entitled "The Tangled Garden". Though not perhaps of great importance in itself, being a simple, decorative tapestry-like study of flowers in a garden, the painting is important in the history of Canadian art as a *cause célèbre*. It was no more and no less than what its title proclaimed; indeed it is remarkable less for formal than for representational qualities, though painted with a lyricism which attests MacDonald's rich competence as a painter. But simply on the grounds of its lively colour and bold design it aroused a barrage of sustained and angry criticism. MacDonald was astonished and a long newspaper controversy ensued, without settling anything. But the hue and cry drew the little band of artists closer together; it placed their names and their work before the public eye; and by making people question accepted standards it gave a considerable stimulus to the new school of painting.

Meanwhile, the First World War had produced Lord Beaverbrook's plan whereby Canadian and other artists of the Commonwealth were chosen to depict the conflict in all its varied phases. The artists selected included Jackson, Lismer, Varley, Milne, Beatty, Forbes and Morrice. In general, they were not turned aside by considerations of patriotic fervour, and painted the struggle as they saw it or interpreted it as they felt it. The result was a fine group of paintings, many of which transcend the documentary. The collection is now in the National Gallery at Ottawa.

After the war was over, the young artists felt that they should formally unite, the better to pursue their common aim. Already, in 1918, Harris, MacDonald and Johnston had begun a series of sketching parties into the wild and rugged Algoma district north of Sault Ste. Marie. Using as their headquarters a box-car of the Algoma Central and Hudson Bay Railway, they penetrated the rounded hills above Lake Superior and the sombre fastnesses of the Agawa Canyon; and beside the rushing waters of the Batchewana and Montreal rivers MacDonald did some of his finest work. In 1920, for the purpose of organizing an exhibition, Carmichael, Harris, Jackson, Johnston, Lismer, MacDonald and Varley formed themselves into a group which was soon dubbed the Group of Seven. It still remains a magic name in Canadian art.

Exhibitions were held each year, and in 1922 the Group issued a manifesto, in which it stated: "Art must take the road and risk all for the glory of a great adventure . . . new material demands new methods, and new methods fling a challenge to old conventions". Fifteen years later, an

English critic, commenting on a retrospective exhibition of works by the Group and its followers noted that, " . . . overtones and undertones may be missed in the search for clarity, and something too near the poster may emerge".

These statements sum up, in simple form, the strength and weakness of the Group's approach. They symbolize its initial enthusiasm and the imitation which followed it. Their dates are perhaps significant: the first was made in the heyday of the Group's activity; the second was made at a time when imitation of the Group's methods, without the central fire, had dulled the edge of creative expression. The years that lie between them constitute an epoch of great importance in the history of our art.

In their various preliminary excursions into the Canadian north, the Group had come to the conclusion that this vast field of new subject matter lent itself to original treatment. "We felt", wrote A. Y. Jackson, a foundation member, and himself occupying a key position in Canadian painting, forming, as it were, a bridge between Morrice and Thomson, "that there was a rich field for landscape *motifs* . . . and we frankly abandoned attempts at literal painting, and treated our subjects with the freedom of the decorative designer. We tried to emphasize colour, line and pattern".

This, then, was their new approach. They realized that the peculiar nature of this Canadian scene, with its gaunt masses of rock, its vivid colours produced by the impetuous rush of the seasons, its clear atmosphere and its sharp surging lines, needed a new approach. The palette of the Impressionists, as modified by Cullen and Morrice, stood ready to hand. This, added to their own enthusiasm, gave them their medium. It was a medium which, while it differed from artist to artist, had certain common factors: strength, sincerity and gusto, strong rhythmic line and swirling pattern, clarity of atmosphere, brilliance of colour, and decorative simplicity and forcefulness. In point of fact, it was profoundly original.

It will be noticed, however, that the terms "design" and "form" are absent from Jackson's pronouncement. These omissions constitute a chink in the Group's armour; and it was through that chink that the forces of imitation entered. With few notable exceptions, there has not been, in the Group's work, that interest in formal values, that complex structural plasticity that seems to have been the end of the greatest art: of Giotto, Michelangelo or Cézanne. The art of the Group was, in a double sense, northern art; it was dynamic line rather than plastic form which interested them. It must also be admitted that the first flush of discovery led to a somewhat romantic and poetic attitude to subject matter, varying from the mysticism of Harris, and the lyricism of MacDonald to the fine poetic fury of Lismer. The members of the Group were conscious crusaders, and their exhibitions were not without deliberate attempts to shock the "old hats". The new subject matter also very naturally led to an emphasis on landscape at the expense of other things; an emphasis on the raw material of Canada rather than on Canadian life.

But the importance of the Group was by no means limited to painting; its members were equally active in other fields. Their enthusiasm, their liveliness in controversy, their progressive ideas, their willingness to defend and encourage younger painters, their vivid interest in all contemporary art and its relation to the public, gave Canadian art a new direction. Their influence is still apparent, either in the form of admiring imitation or angry revolt, in much of our contemporary painting. The Group's importance lies as much in this, as in its achievements in paint and canvas. During the twenties and early thirties its members were a source of inspiration to scores of younger artists. Some of them taught, and their ideas quickly spread in an ever-widening circle. They travelled and painted throughout Canada: the Rockies, the Pacific Coast, the Lower St. Lawrence, the Maritimes, and Northern Ontario from the north shore of Lake Superior to Georgian Bay and Algonquin Park. And if these varied regions sometimes seemed, in their canvases, curiously alike, the decade of the twenties yet saw a vital juice coursing through the arteries of Canadian painting.

The zenith of the Group's achievement occurred during the years 1924-1927, and is underlined by the immediate and stimulating success of the Canadian art exhibitions at London in 1924-1925 and at Paris in 1927. Here their dash, brilliant colour and decorative ability found a ready response among critics and public alike.

"Emphatic design and bold brushwork . . . bold simplification", said *The Times*. "A fine decorative sense and a passionate preoccupation with the stress of growth", said the *Saturday Review*. "Here are people with something vital to say", remarked the *New York News*, "who say it well and with emphasis, and at the same time with a typically Canadian outlook". And again *The Times*, "to anybody who conceives of a picture as a decorative construction in paint, the landscapes . . . cannot fail to give satisfaction". There is the crux of the matter. Granted its premises, the Group fulfilled its aesthetic canons; but these very canons sometimes shackled its members unduly. "Their bold decorative landscapes, emphasizing colour, line and pattern, give the very look and feel of Canada . . . Young artists painting a young country superbly through their temperaments, not literally . . . standing on their own feet, revealing their own country with gay virility", said the *Daily Chronicle*.

Johnston had resigned in 1922, but the others had added to their ranks. A. J. Casson, a water-colourist, joined in

1926, E. H. Holgate of Montreal in 1931, and L. L. Fitz-gerald of Winnipeg in 1932. These, together with invited contributors, held an exhibition almost every year until 1933, when the Group merged with the larger Canadian Group of Painters. In the interval MacDonald had died in 1932.

Though bound by common beliefs, each member had his individual style; and recent retrospective exhibitions of their work have made it possible to re-assess its value. The four giants are quite evidently Jackson, Harris, MacDonald and Lismer. It is impossible to look at forty years of their painting spread out on gallery walls without experiencing a sense of very solid achievement.

Jackson proved himself the more subtle colourist, due possibly to the influence of Morrice; and as he progressed, his colour and form both loosened up, and he achieved re-sults at once more complex and more effortless than in his earlier canvases. In his late sixties he extended his search for the essence of the Canadian scene to Yellowknife, Great Bear Lake and the valley of the Mackenzie; and his later paintings have a sweep and authority which confirm his position as Canada's leading landscape painter.

With Lismer it is the struggle for realization which ex-cites: the genuine *furor poeticus*. He is extraordinarily uneven, but never dull. His Georgian Bay and Maritime canvases sparkle with fire and gaiety. In his turbulent, gusty paintings he comes closer than anyone else to the giant rhythms and the heaving fecundity of the earth. Into his world-renowned work in the field of art education for children he has carried the same vivid and unpredictable enthusiasms.

Harris, to whose generosity the Group owed so much, produced highly simplified work, tending toward abstrac-tion. Its solemn grandeur gave an added solidity to the common style which, in general, was more concerned with

61

the flow of line and pattern; but his approach led him inevitably into the field of non-objective art. Yet his massive, austere and gloomy paintings of a land carved in the grand manner are strangely impressive, whether the subject be an Arctic island, a Lake Superior sunset or a lighthouse on the Lower St. Lawrence.

MacDonald is a majestic lyricist. He combines delicate colour with broad, bold forms, and envelops the whole in an atmosphere which can only be described as mystical. His work may vary from the solemn splendour of a towering Algoma hillside to the flicker of a fallen leaf on a quiet beaver dam. His excursions into Impressionism may have weakened his rich lyricism; but in his pearly sketches this becomes an advantage, and they glow with vitality and spontaneity.

Varley's excellence as a portraitist lies in his ability to combine the decorative approach with a feeling for modelling and the values of related tones. In landscape, this enabled him to capture, with suave assurance, the atmosphere of the mountains of the Pacific Coast. Fitzgerald specialized in delicate, feathery drawings and oils, created with slow, contemplative sureness. The nudes and figure work of Holgate are conceived with authority, and he also achieved telling effects in the graphic arts.

The highly patterned water-colours of Carmichael and Casson, showing plainly the influence of their training as commercial designers, gave added strength to a medium which had languished. It was due largely to their efforts and those of C. W. Jefferys, F. H. Brigden and Peter Haworth, that the Canadian Society of Painters in Water-Colour was formed in 1926 and progressed so swiftly.

During the decade 1923-1933 the influence of the Group spread and a number of painters appeared, all of whom owed much to its approach and followed it closely. The more outstanding are L. A. C. Panton, Yvonne McKague Housser, Kathleen Daly, Dorothy Stevens and Isobel McLaughlin in Ontario; Albert Robinson, Prudence Heward and Anne Savage in Quebec; and J. W. G. MacDonald in British Columbia. The work of some of these painters will be discussed later. Each had his own style and each tended to make a special preserve of subject matter which he undertook to interpret. As the topographers had recorded an older Canada, these artists recorded the newer Canada: mining towns on the Shield, pulp mills, mountain peaks, and fishing villages.

Parallel to their efforts, older painters who solved their problems along more individual lines were also at work. The most important are Emily Carr and David Milne. Emily Carr is one of the handful of undeniably great painters which this country has produced. A lonely, intense and monolithic personality, working in obscurity in Victoria, B.C., she created vivid and unforgettable images of the British Columbia forest and of Indian life. In her swirling canvases of greens and greys and vivid blues the forest comes to life: the great trees send their supplicating arms skyward and the new growth burgeons and races across the forest floor. Emily Carr worked with a frenzied brush; but the frenzy was rigidly controlled by a deeply rooted sense of order, so that her paintings continually surprise with their dramatic but contained excitement.

Vastly different, but no whit less original, is the work of David Milne. In his dry, almost laconic oils and his limpid economical water-colours he has created, in landscape and still life, a world of line, pattern and tone, within an astonishingly narrow colour range. As his art progressed it became at once freer and more calligraphic, so that a few deceptively simple lines and areas of tone may sum up a canoe on a northern lake; an arrangement of flowers, old jam

63

jars and paper boxes may assume the quality of a latter-day
Chardin; and a city street can become a scene of haunting,
floodlit mystery.

At the same time, water-colour and the graphic media
were undergoing a rapid transformation, and a group of
Sunday painters spread the gospel of Canadianism far and
wide. But while amateurs occasionally achieved professional
rank, as in the case of Bertram Brooker, whose contribution
to graphic art and illustration was both original and striking,
there also grew up the feeling that almost anyone could be
a painter. The various societies did not hesitate to admit
to their ranks and to their exhibitions those whose approach
and style, as well as their status, were not only amateur but
amateurish. This in turn meant that critics did not scruple
to applaud local talent, simply because it was local; and
that the public, lacking guidance, was sometimes unable to
discern the difference between a dedicated professional and
a benign dabbler. The curse of the amateur lies heavy on
the era which saw the end of the existence of the Group of
Seven as a formal association.

This took place in 1933, and it co-incided with a falling
off in quality, and a period of indecision not unconnected
with the depression. The reason for this is not far to seek.
The Group, whatever its artistic limitations, had been animated by a tremendous vitality. But the history of art has
shown that when such a group emerges, its followers all too
frequently imitate its approach, its methods, even its mannerisms, without the fire of their masters. This was precisely
what happened in Canada. It was a normal occurrence
and should not be a cause for regret. During the years up
to 1933 it became increasingly evident that the manner of
the Group was being followed so widely and so closely, that
a blight was in danger of settling on Canadian art: a blight
fully as tenacious and unfruitful as a transplanted academi-

cism, or the old inspiration of the decadent Dutch and neo-Barbizon schools.

Had the Group's artistic approach been as unexceptionable as its crusading spirit, this might not have mattered. But such was not the case. As the eminent critic, Jean Chauvin, has pointed out:

"Les peintres du Group des Sept voulurent libérer la peinture canadienne des théories du clasicisme européen et des dernières attaches qui la retenaient à l'impressionisme et au pointillisme. Malheureusement, la matière de ces peintres est une manière inféconde, étroite, dont on a vite fait le tour. Comme technique, c'est excellent pour la composition, la décoration, la fresque et l'affiche. Mais, comme trop de peintres de ce mouvement s'arrêtent à la surface des objets et des choses, ce sont, pour les débutants du moins, de mauvais maîtres".

This is a hard judgement, but it is also realistic; and none was quicker to sense the needs of the situation than the Group of Seven itself. In 1933 it ceased to exist and merged with the newly formed Canadian Group of Painters, in the hope that enthusiasm and creative originality would supplant the imitation of now empty forms. Further, MacDonald had died the previous year, and the end of a chapter was in sight. The Group had left behind a tradition of *pleinairiste* drama and conflict, and a rebellious creative spirit; it had aroused enthusiasm among the public and fostered independence of outlook among the artists. For close to twenty years it had dominated the Canadian scene.

This statement, however, needs qualification: it was the English-speaking Canadian scene which had been dominated. It is significant that the first really objective critical assessment of the Group's work was made in Montreal; for it was there that contemporary painting was later to get its second wind. French-speaking artists, with memories of their own great tradition, were to revolt against both the manner and the matter of the Canadian landscape school, and to produce an art no less dynamic, and a good deal more subtle.

CHAPTER VIII

Art Broadens Its Base
1885-1940

IN ANCIENT LANDS the possession of an artistic tradition
eventually gives rise to the foundation of institutions, galleries and societies which may variously guard its treasures,
enshrine its canons or systematize its beliefs. In younger
countries the process is usually reversed and, as we noted
in an earlier chapter, the Royal Canadian Academy and
the National Gallery of Canada were created at a time
when our national art was in an embryonic stage. Thereafter, however, art and its institutions developed along
roughly parallel lines.

The number of societies, institutions, associations,
galleries and educational bodies connected with our art
increased enormously during the period under review. It
is neither possible nor desirable to deal with them all sepa-
rately, since many of them were of importance only in the
sense that they were symbols of a more active interest in
art at the community level. However, it will be well to
mention the more important of these bodies, since a number
of them owe their existence to the encouragement of the
National Gallery.

In the Maritimes the period was marked by little save
the establishment of the Owens Art Gallery at Mount Allison University, in New Brunswick, and of the Provincial
Archives in Nova Scotia. But in 1932 the New Brunswick
Museum was re-organized, and in 1935 the National Gallery
helped in the formation of the Maritime Art Association.
With Professor Walter Abell, of Acadia University, as its

first president, this body organized travelling exhibitions, and founded the magazine *Maritime Art,* which later developed into the national periodical *Canadian Art.* This journal is still the only one to be devoted exclusively to a general survey of the progress of the visual arts in Canada.

In Quebec, the Art Association of Montreal, though formed in 1860, was for many years a passive repository of mediocre European painting. But by the mid-thirties, the collection had been thinned and a number of fine works by Canadian and foreign artists acquired. The building was enlarged, children's classes were initiated, the school of art was reorganized and the whole institution placed on a much more active basis.

The Musée Provincial at Quebec City built up a collection of valuable historical material and also acquired an excellent body of work by contemporary French-speaking artists, including some of the so-called Primitives of the Murray Bay region. The permanent collection at Laval University is of considerable interest to both the connoisseur and the art historian.

In Ontario, the management of the Canadian National Exhibition in Toronto added an art gallery to its collection of permanent buildings; and though it is typical of the period immediately prior to the First World War that the names GIOTTO and ALMA-TADEMA should have adorned adjacent niches in its walls, it has been the scene of a number of major exhibitions. In playing host to an audience of millions the exhibition committee was naturally concerned to provide a good drawing card; but in the years leading up to the Second World War, large exhibitions of British, French, American and Canadian art were successfully displayed.

In 1900 the Art Museum of Toronto, subsequently renamed the Art Gallery, was founded. It grew steadily, expanded its fine building, acquired a permanent collection of very considerable value, and, largely through the work of Arthur Lismer, gained an international reputation in the field of art education. Twelve years later the Royal Ontario Museum of Archaeology was established, and its collection of Chinese ceramics and bronzes is now one of the finest on the continent. In 1913 the first *Yearbook of the Arts* was published. It was a modest affair, and is interesting today less for critical than for historical information; but its successors of 1929 and 1936, edited by Bertram Brooker, were more mature in tone. More recent years saw the growth of local societies, the formation of art associations, the extension of art education through the various technical and vocational schools, and the further development of the Ontario College of Art.

On the prairies, the formation of the Winnipeg Art Gallery and its co-operation with the University of Manitoba and the Winnipeg School of Art were helpful beginnings in a city usually identified in the public mind with musical activities. Saskatchewan came forward, in the late thirties, with a programme including a course in fine art at the University, with a practical laboratory in the Mackenzie Foundation collection at Regina. In Alberta, the Edmonton Museum of Arts was opened in the late twenties; and in the thirties, the University of Alberta summer school at Banff began to build its solid reputation as a training ground for enthusiasts.

On the Pacific Coast, a loan exhibition from the National Gallery resulted in the formation of the British Columbia Art League; and in the depths of the depression, the generosity of its citizens enabled Vancouver to build a fine art gallery. A little earlier the Vancouver School of Art, under the direction of Charles H. Scott, had opened its doors.

An important development during the late thirties was the establishment of departments of fine art at the universities of Toronto, McMaster, Saskatchewan and Acadia, and the appointment of resident artists at Queen's and Mount Allison. Excellent work was begun in creating a reservoir of trained museum and gallery workers and, in the case of the University of Toronto, and later, McGill, courses were established leading to the granting of a degree in fine arts.

This brief summary will have indicated that an interest in art is a cumulative process depending on artist and public alike; and the part played by the National Gallery in this process should not be overlooked. During the twenties and thirties the Gallery built up the finest collection of European painting in the country; but this was only one side of its programme. In common with other art museums in Canada, the Gallery recognized its educational responsibilities, and one of its most successful ventures was the travelling exhibition of Canadian art, circulating throughout the nation and available to any institution or group that might wish to sponsor it.

Other events which influenced public opinion in the period between the wars were the Canadian exhibitions held abroad and sponsored by the Gallery. Chief among them were those at London in 1924 and 1925, at Paris in 1927, at Buenos Aires in 1931, at Johannesburg in 1936-1937, "A Century of Canadian Art" at London in 1938, and a series of major exhibitions at the New York World's Fair in 1939. These activities were supplemented by annual showings of Canadian art at home and by loan exhibitions of foreign art. In co-operation with the Canadian Committee of the Carnegie Corporation the Gallery also initiated a system of training for those intending to take up museum work, while lecture tours by Canadian and foreign authorities were frequently sponsored. In any estimate of the development of public interest in the visual arts, the name of the National Gallery necessarily bulks large. Being a federal institution, it saw in terms of the country as a whole; it also saw in terms of the future and did not hesitate to acquire works by promising young Canadians when, to do so, was often to incur the displeasure of official artists' organizations.

CHAPTER IX

*Quebec: A Fresh Approach
1938-1950*

T HE GROUP OF SEVEN, while it developed into a national movement, was essentially based on the city of Toronto. It found both its critics and its supporters in that inscrutable city which, while enjoying a not entirely ill-deserved opprobrium in the rest of Canada for its complacency, had nevertheless long held leadership in the visual arts. But in making Toronto its headquarters, the Group necessarily cut itself off from the traditions and the heritage of French-speaking Canadians. Its devotion to pure landscape would, in any case, have rendered such a course inescapable. For while members of the group ranged far and wide throughout the Province of Quebec in their search for *motifs,* it was external appearances, rather than the inward painting of the mind which chiefly concerned them.

It is true that this approach made a considerable impact on Montreal; but it was on the Montreal that lies west of Boulevard St. Laurent. The Beaver Hall Group of English-speaking painters, under the leadership of Edwin Holgate, became the Montreal wing of this enthusiastic discovery of the Canadian landscape; and the followers of the Group of Seven numbered many distinguished painters. Albert Robinson developed a simplified, quietist attitude which owed perhaps as much to Morrice as to the inspiration of his Toronto colleagues. The limpid, lyric rhythms of Anne Savage, the bright, loosely-painted city scenes of Sarah

Robertson, and the somewhat aloof statements of Kathleen Morris, also announced a common source.

Three painters who generated their ideas in this atmosphere each struck out on individual lines: Prudence Heward, Lilias Torrance Newton and Marian Scott. Prudence Heward, interested from the first in applying the bold, broad technique of the Group to figure work and portraits-in-a-landscape, developed an intense and sombre feeling for the human figure. Her portrait studies of children and young girls, instinct with a powerful melancholy and painted in the round, grew ever freer and more boldly plastic. Lilias Newton, adapting the pure colour and flat areas of the Group to a more sophisticated and personal approach, became Canada's leading portraitist. Her simplified use of bold planes enabled her to effect subtle characterizations and to take the curse off "official" portraiture. Marian Scott turned her eye inward to the world revealed in the structure of flowers, vegetables and shells. She explored this hidden world with ever greater certainty until she achieved, as in her mural on endocrinology at McGill University, the distinction of making intricate and compelling abstractions out of the very cells of which life is composed.

Yet it was not possible that the naïve exuberance of discovery should wholly appeal to a city and to a people whose tradition in the plastic arts was so strong. Such an approach smacked always in Montreal of a quasi-alien culture; and it was unlikely to succeed in the city of James Wilson Morrice. Even while the Group of Seven was making headlines, it was treated here with some reserve; and many Montreal artists suspended judgement. As one of them, John Lyman, succinctly put it: "This talk of the Canadian scene has gone sour; the real Canadian scene is in the consciousness of Canadian painters, whatever the object of their thought".

Lyman, who had known Morrice and admired his work, and who had himself studied with Matisse in France, was unlikely, with his subtler attitude toward painting, to view the direct and sometimes brassy technique of the Group of Seven with anything but a slightly jaundiced eye. On his return to Montreal from France in the early thirties, and being a writer and an organizer as well as an artist, he set to work to campaign for an approach which would concern itself more with the problems of painting than with those of subject matter. He became art critic for *The Montrealer* and later founded the Contemporary Art Society. Its showings included the work of a number of artists who, both in their names and in their attitudes, testified to the cosmopolitan nature of Canada's largest city, and sometimes made the Toronto group appear a shade provincial.

Fritz Brandtner used the acid colours and sharp contours of the German Expressionists to delineate city streets, docks, factories, and a newer, more violent Laurentian landscape. Aleksandre Bercovitch and Samuel Borenstein brought a love of bright colour and richer paint to the plastic handling of figure work and city scenes. Louis Muhlstock developed delicate and sensitive studies of nudes in charcoal, and later expanded his notable talent to rich, sunny, freshly painted oils of the city and its parks. Eric Goldberg's delicate and gossamer-like sophistication sometimes seemed like Saladin's scimitar beside the broadsword of the followers of the Group of Seven.

Among French-speaking Canadians, Marc-Aurèle Fortin explored the topography of Montreal in loose, slashing water colours, or painted, with something of the richness of stained glass, the enormous elms and crumbling old manor houses along the banks of the Rivière des Prairies. Adrien Hébert painted quiet and restrained landscapes; while in Quebec, Jean-Paul Lemieux, at times a conscious "primitive", de-

74

veloped with extreme charm a little private but quite
accessible series of miracle plays in paint along the Lower
St. Lawrence.

But it was not until the return of Alfred Pellan from
France in 1939 that the younger generation of Montreal
painters found a spokesman who, in addition to being something of an *enfant terrible,* was also a virtuoso sufficiently
gifted to convince them that what was needed to offset the
now respectable enthusiasm of the Group of Seven was the
adaptation of the discoveries of the School of Paris to the
traditional Quebec skill in the plastic arts.

The movement was launched by the critics with full
gallic fervour. It included readings out of the party, and
death (more or less) by ostracism, to deviationists, academes
and regionalists. The young camp-followers regarded
Pellan as their champion, and Lyman as a benevolent uncle;
and they emerged from the studios and the Ecole des Beaux
Arts with a determination to found their own school. This
intention, aided and abetted by the writers, was as deliberate
and as well publicized as the Group of Seven's had been
twenty years earlier. But in the case of the Montrealers, the
masters were to be, not the rock and the lake and the pine,
but the smouldering violence of Rouault, the limpid colour
and incomparable slithery line of Matisse, and the sure-
footed acrobatics of Picasso.

The impact made on Canadian art by this group was
very considerable, as no doubt will be the impact made on
their followers by new groups that will arise later on. These
periodic convulsions are an index of the healthy state of
any nation's art; and certainly the pendulum, during the
twenties and thirties, had swung too far in the direction
of "Canadian" subject matter. The Montreal group re-
dressed the balance; and their achievement as painters is
certainly impressive.

75

Pellan himself was perhaps too great a virtuoso for his own good. His determination to shock and surprise was sometimes apt to end by becoming itself provincial; because what caused raised eyebrows in Montreal had often been *vieux jeu* in Paris since the Cubists had exhibited before the First World War. But Pellan's personality was electric, and his painting superb. He is a craftsman with an uncanny feeling for line, a sense of colour at once esoteric and bold, and an intellectual vigour which, allied to a sure hand and a shrewd eye, have enabled him to run the gamut of abstraction, cubism, surrealism and fauvism among a people traditionally gifted in the plastic arts. With his example to guide them, and taking advantage of the revival of interest in fine book production and the applied arts, the group became at once an attitude and an achievement. A series of booklets on its members was produced by a Montreal publishing house, and it secured the approbation of the dean of Montreal critics, Jean Chauvin.

Of the group of artists which rose to fame on this veritable renaissance of painting in Quebec, the most outstanding represent, fittingly, Canada's two great races. They are Paul-Emile Borduas, Goodridge Roberts, Stanley Cosgrove and Jacques de Tonnancour. The art of Borduas is dark, intense and explosive. He is concerned with the inward eye, and his thickly painted sombre abstractions have something of the passion of an Oroszco; though they are, to the general public, perhaps more difficult of access. In Goodridge Roberts, the inward eye is mellowed by a genuine feeling for the lyric element. His landscapes are extremely rich and satisfying; and his sensuous use of paint blends the rolling hills of the Eastern Townships into the harmonious patterns of an art sufficiently representational to be pleasing even to those who may miss the easy smoothness of his paint. Stanley Cosgrove proclaims his debt both to the

School of Paris and to the modern Mexican painters. His master, initially, was Braque; and his still lifes and figure painting have both the sensitiveness to design and the aloof quality of his master. Jacques de Tonnancour, the youngest of the four, is still in the process of finding himself. He has a vivid sense of linear composition, great delicacy of expression and a firm yet light touch in his use of colour which makes his still lifes, portraiture and landscapes at once subtle and distinctive.

Subtlety indeed, as opposed to directness, is the hall-mark of most of the contemporary Montreal painters. Their concern with manner at the expense of matter marks them off sharply from those who still feel that the bones of the Canadian landscape are what makes a painting live. This subtlety may take the form of the mystery and nostalgia of streets at night, as with Philip Surrey; it may assume the suave understatement of Alan Harrison; the unerring sense of design which produces the deceptive simplicity of Henry Eveleigh; or the intimate qualities of Chicoine and Gauvreau. It may even be apparent in the wiry lines and cunningly placed washes which mark the water-colours of Jori Smith; or the intricate and evocative spider's web drawings of Oscar Cahen, a notable illustrator of magazines and periodicals.

On the other hand such painters as Jean-Charles Faucher, drawing on the simple patterns of the so-called Murray Bay Primitives (those untutored Sunday painters recently discovered by our neighbours across the border), have been both naïve and direct. The difference of course is that Faucher's directness is considered and sophisticated, whereas the directness of the Group of Seven was—direct.

There remains Robert La Palme, who stoutly refuses to fit into any category. His outrageously grotesque and amusing distortions of the human figure, whether they adorn the editorial page of the French language daily *Le Canada,* or whether they burst across a wall in the form of a vivid and violent mural, are at once the most irrepressible kind of painting and genuine public pamphleteering. La Palme is a wit who has restored the art of caricature to the high place which it enjoyed in the days of Henri Julien. His notable series, "The History of Medicine" and "The History of Warfare" proclaim him to be a social historian of the most devastating kind; a sort of twentieth-century Quebec Cruikshank or Gillray.

The lively advance of this Montreal group undoubtedly owed something to the Second World War, since, after the fall of France in 1940, Montreal, along with Rio de Janeiro, became for some time the leading centre of publication in the French language. Illustrators, typographers and artists found fresh and stimulating employment; and this in turn encouraged Montreal publishers to undertake more venturesome work. The paintings of the group were at first but little noticed outside Montreal; in fact they received their first major accolade at a series of notable exhibitions arranged in Brazil by the National Gallery of Canada, during the tenure of office as ambassador of M. Jean Désy, a man of wide culture and undoubted promotional talents.

When their fame spread to the rest of Canada it restored a balance between subject matter and approach. Not only did these painters uncover the well-springs of the French-Canadian tradition and beget a new interest in handicrafts, ecclesiastical decoration and the paintings of such half-forgotten artists as Ozias Leduc and Antoine Plamondon; their work also co-incided with a possibly subconscious recognition among Canadians, made articulate by their artists, that the nation no longer had to insist on its vigorous independence through an exclusive devotion to typically Canadian subject matter. That battle had been fought twenty years earlier. Canadian artists could now turn to full self-expression, knowing that the Canadian atmosphere and heritage had struck their roots so deep that they would be evident, as a distinctive approach, no matter what the style or manner of their painters.

CHAPTER X

The Artists of the Second World War

IT IS ONE of the mysteries of human activity that in moments of crisis we can perform feats of endurance and imagination which are not possible during normal times. The arts are no exception. The first rich upsurge of Dutch painting came hard on the heels of the liberation of the Low Countries from the Spanish yoke; the finest of contemporary Mexican art was the product of a bitter social revolution; and the United States found itself at its most volubly native in the depths of the depression.

It is a commonplace that the recent growth of Canada to full national stature was immeasurably hastened by the Second World War and its aftermath; and the nation was fortunate in finding, to record its supreme moments, some of the most gifted of its contemporary painters. They interpreted, with an artist's unique and personal insight, not merely the outward seeming but the inner meaning of the great struggle in which the nation was engaged.

It may seem at first sight a paradox that a brilliant artist like Charles Comfort should be at home amid the impersonal and monolithic shapes of mechanized warfare; that a cool and intimate landscapist like Carl Schaefer should find himself equally at ease in a Lancaster bomber; or that subtle and sensitive figure painters like Will Ogilvie and Jack Nichols should grasp the essentials of human relationships in the tank corps or aboard a destroyer. Yet an artist's eye remains personal to him, no matter what the object of its gaze; and the Canadian War Artists achieved a resounding imaginative success in their documentation of the great struggle.

The employment of War Artists for the Canadian Armed Forces was agreed to in October, 1942, after earlier representations by the National Gallery and by Rt. Hon. Vincent Massey, at that time High Commissioner for Canada in the United Kingdom. A committee under the chairmanship of the Adjutant-General, and composed of personnel heads of the three services, studied the method of selecting artists, their status in the services and the direction of their activities. Their recommendations received government approval at the end of 1942.

A Selection Committee was formed under the chairmanship of Mr. H. O. McCurry, Director of the National Gallery, and consisting of the Navy Historian, the Director, Historical Section (Army) and the Air Historian. This committee was to direct the activities of the artists in Canada, while a Canadian Overseas Artists Control Committee was set up in London, consisting of the High Commissioner for Canada and the senior officers of the three services. In practice, the work of the artists was directed by the historical sections of the three services.

Behind this rather formidable array of committees lay a genuine desire, fostered by Mr. Massey, and heartily concurred in by the heads of the armed forces, to give the artist as unfettered a rein as might be consistent with security; and to ensure that, in directing him to record the exploits of the armed forces, he was not unduly confined in his movements or made to adhere to rigid specifications in his art. It was a sensible course to take.

In the Army overseas, artists were alternated between the field and an improvised studio in London. They would spend several months sketching in the theatre of operations—Sicily, Italy or Normandy—and then several months in London developing their sketches into larger works. The artists were carried on the Field Historical Sections, and the Army eventually had at the headquarters of every fighting division a team composed of an historical officer and a war artist, with their own transport and equipment. Somewhat similar plans were followed by both the Navy and the Air Force.

The original scheme provided for three artists in the Navy, and six each in the Army and the Air Force. Early in 1944 this plan was revised to increase the number to six for the Navy and ten each for the Army and the Air Force. Artists could be promoted to the rank of Captain (Army) or equivalent, after a year of service, with the provision that not more than two in each service could be promoted to the rank of Major or equivalent. All the materials used by the artists were bought at public expense, and all their paintings became the property of the government. It is unlikely that the government ever made a better investment.

The war artists painted in all parts of Canada and recorded activities on the home front and in training establishments and factories; they flew in bomber raids over Germany; they dramatized the heat of the Italian and Normandy campaigns; and they sailed in destroyers in convoy on the Atlantic and on the Narrow Seas. All of them served with distinction, and a number of them were decorated for feats concerned less with the plastic arts than with the arts of war. In the list which follows, the average Canadian art lover may now find it strange to see a half-forgotten service rank preceding the name of a well-known artist: but it was in such rank that their work was done, and that in this particular context it best deserves to be remembered. The following were the artists employed:

Royal Canadian Navy: Commander Harold Beament, V.D.; Lt.-Commander C. A. Law, D.S.C.; Lt. Donald Mackay; Lt. Jack Nichols; Lt. Rowley Murphy; Lt. Michael Forster; Lt. Tom Wood; Lt. Leonard Brooks.

Canadian Army: Major Charles F. Comfort; Major Will Ogilvie, M.B.E.; Capt. Bruno Bobak; Capt. D. A. Colville; Capt. Orville Fisher; Capt. Lawren P. Harris; Capt. E. J. Hughes; Capt. George Pepper; Capt. Campbell Tinning; Lt. Molly Lamb Bobak; Lt. T. R. MacDonald.

Royal Canadian Air Force: F/L Eric Aldwinckle; F/O. D. K. Anderson; F/L A. Bayefsky; F/L Miller Brittain, D.F.C.; F/L Albert Cloutier; F/L P. G. Cowley-Brown; F/L Charles Goldhamer; F/L Paul Goranson; F/O Edwin H. Holgate; F/L R. S. Hyndman; F/O Maurice Reinblatt; F/O Goodridge Roberts; F/L Carl Schaefer.

These artists would never have been precisely so described in the services, since initials, rather than given names, are the rule. But a combination of the rank and the given name may perhaps serve to underline the civilian-turned-soldier and the artist-turned-seaman aspects of their work, as well as its essential freedom and unfettered approach.

The group may be divided into those well-established artists who adapted their talents to fresh subject matter; and those who found themselves through their activities as war artists. Not all the work produced was above the pedestrian, but certain painters developed astonishingly.

Charles Comfort had long been one of the most accomplished of our contemporary artists. With an uncanny skill in the handling of paint, he produced unexpected textures and vivid impressions in which his vision was stripped to its bare essentials. He also possessed a striking sense of the dramatic. In such major works as his murals for the Toronto Stock Exchange and the International Nickel Company, he had shown a marked capacity for integrating, in simplified painting shorthand, the forms of men and machines. This talent was now developed to a high degree in his work with the Army; and his paintings of the Italian campaign have a vivid and dramatic immediacy which far transcends their documentary value.

His companion in arms, Will Ogilvie, adapted a loving sense of delicate figure composition and a sure lyric line (notable in his mural for the chapel of Hart House, University of Toronto) to the needs of his new profession. His campaign paintings, and especially his sketches and portraits of army types are filled with humanity; while his art acquired, in these new surroundings, an added firmness and authority.

Lawren P. Harris, son of a distinguished father, succeeded in creating, in his highly enamelled paintings, a nightmare, quasi-surrealist world where the indifference of mechanical shapes to the men who operate them was stated with a classic simplicity. George Pepper and Edwin Holgate, painters in the tradition of the Group of Seven, created many sturdy sketches; while Orville Fisher's early training in the graphic media enabled him to produce vivid impressions of the Normandy campaign.

In the Navy, Tom Wood and Leonard Brooks found themselves at home in action scenes, both gusty and sensitive; while Michael Forster's sombre semi-abstract studies of naval life, especially the shapes of submarines in pens or of ships at sea and at rest, created the same sense of calm intensity that one finds in the work of the English artist, Eric Ravilious.

J. W. Morrice: THE FERRY, QUEBEC

Tom Thomson: SPRING ICE

Photo: Richard Harrington

Haida Totem Pole, Queen Charlotte Islands, B.C.

J-B Côté: The Last Supper

The Royal Ontario Museum of Archaeology

The Art Gallery of Toronto; prese...
Walter C. Laidl...

Paul Labrosse (attribute...
Virgin and Child

ᴄʜᴀᴛᴇᴀᴜ ᴅᴇ Rᴀᴍᴇᴢᴀʏ, Mᴏɴᴛʀᴇᴀʟ

Photo: Editorial Associates

ᴡᴏᴏᴅᴇɴ Cʀᴜᴄɪꜰɪx, by an unknown 18th-
tury woodcarver in the Richelieu Valley

Collection: M. Jean Palardy, Montreal

Cʜᴜʀᴄʜ, Sᴛᴇ. Fᴀᴍɪʟʟᴇ, Iʟᴇ ᴅ'Oʀʟᴇᴀɴs

Photo: Professor Ramsay Traquair

Captain Herbert Warre: THE
CASCADE MOUNTAINS

The Public Archives of Canada

Cornelius Krieghoff: MERRYMA

John T. Ross Collection, Quebe

Paul Kane: INDIAN ENCAMP

The Art Gallery of Toronto

Homer Watson: THE FLOOD GATE

The National Gallery of Canada

The National Gallery of Canada

J. E. H. MacDonald: GLEAMS ON THE HILLS

F. H. Varley: GEORGIAN BA

The National Gallery of Canada

Arthur Lismer: ROCK, PINE
SUNLIGHT

The Art Gallery of Toront

André Biéler: GATINEAU MADONNA

The National Gallery of Canada

Jack Humphrey: JOANNE

The National Gallery of Canada

A. Y. Jackson: ALGOMA, NOVEMBER

David B. Milne: RITES OF AUTUMN

The National Gallery of Canada

Lawren S. Harris: Afternoon Sun, Lake Superior

The National Gallery of Canada

Goodridge Roberts: Lake Orford

P-E Borduas: LA TAHITIENNE

Collection: M. Luc Choquette, Montreal

Henri Masson: LANDSCAPE,
IRONSIDES, P.Q.

The National Gallery of Canada

Stanley Cosgrove: STILL L

The National Gallery of Cana

cques de Tonnancour: Head of a Woman

llection: H. S. Southam, Esq., C. M. G., Ottawa

ed Pellan: Still Life

n: Dr. Paul Dumas, Montreal

Canadian War Collection: National Gallery of Canada

Jack Nichols: Eight to Twelve Watch on Convoy

Charles F. Comfort
Headquarters of a Light
Aircraft Troop

Canadian War Collecti
National Gallery of Can

Carl Schaefer: BULL'S EYE, NIGHT EXERCISES, SURREY

Robert La Palme: LES AMAZONES

Emanuel Hahn: DESIGN FOR SILVER DOLLAR

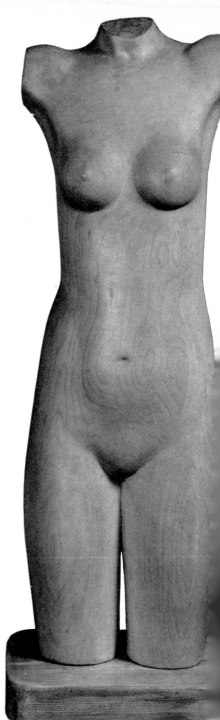

Florence Wyle: YOUNG AMAZ

Armand Filion: TETE DE FA

abeth Wyn Wood: LELAWALA, LEGEND OF NIAGARA

Courtesy of the Artist

Frances Loring: THE REFUGEES

Courtesy of the Artist

BUS SHELTER FOR THE TORONTO TRANS-
PORTATION COMMISSION

John B. Parkin & Associates

SOUTH PLANT OF THE ALUMINUM
COMPANY OF CANADA, Kingston, Ont.

J. C. Meadowcroft and Mathers & Haldenby
Courtesy of the Aluminum Company of
Canada. Photo: R.A.I.C. Journal

TERMINAL GRAIN ELEVATOR,
Arthur, Ont.

Photo: Editorial Associates

With the R.C.A.F., Miller Brittain, a biting but humane social satirist from the Maritimes, found new subjects for his trenchant brush in the battles of the air. Goodridge Roberts turned his lyric talent to the rendering of air force occasions. Carl Schaefer, who had long hymned the saga of rich Ontario farmlands and grotesque Ontario farm-houses, now created sober and dramatic paintings patterned with the ominous forms of assembled bombers, or the flare of flak on the Berlin run.

Of the younger artists, the most outstanding in retrospect seem to have been Jack Nichols, E. J. Hughes and Molly Lamb Bobak. Nichols is perhaps the finest figure painter among our contemporary artists. Working in charcoal, pencil, ink and wash, with thick expressive lines and delicate shadings creating form in the round, his deep sense of humanity had found its subjects among the slums of Toronto. The same human tragedy, dignity and pathos emerged, in even more striking form, in a wonderful series of studies aboard destroyers and corvettes. Groups of sailors in the sick bay, in their hammocks in the foetid below-decks atmosphere of a pitching destroyer, or snatching a few brief moments of leisure in the heat and press of convoy duty: all these convey both the sadness and the ultimate serenity of a scene from Dostoievsky. Nichols is still in his twenties, and with a Guggenheim Fellowship behind him, bids fair to become our leading exponent of the still sad music of humanity.

It was perhaps from the primitives that E. J. Hughes adapted the direct style which made his scenes of the Aleutian campaign and on the Pacific Coast documents of great vividness, and of a curious and perhaps unconscious irony. His groups of soldiers in training or on parade have the quality of protesting cyphers caught in the machine, and are thus in the great tradition of war comment.

85

With Molly Lamb Bobak it is simply a question of being endowed with an irrepressible exuberance and a complete self-assurance which enable her to attack her subject with a fresh and disarming enthusiasm—let the paint fall where it may. Though her work is sometimes confused and often wayward, it has great gusto and undoubted charm. To record their activities, the Canadian Women's Army Corps could scarcely have wished for a more sympathetic, if unorthodox chronicler.

If the Canadian War Artists are considered on the basis of their terms of reference, their record is excellent: a permanent and vivid commentary, seen through the eyes of sensitive painters, on a great national effort. But beyond this, they may be considered simply as artists. Here, the development of their own work, and the feeling that the struggle was painted with skilled craftsmanship and vision, rather than with any avowed nationalist philosophy, will perhaps rank as their greatest contribution to the development of our art.

CHAPTER XI

Contemporary Painting

THE TWO MAIN STREAMS of contemporary painting hitherto examined have by no means exhausted the catalogue of significant painters who have maintained a separate course. As in the art of most countries, there are always some painters who defy the tendency of the historian to classify, and whose work, taken as a body, constitutes a distinguished output.

As yet, the number of painters who earn their living solely through their work is limited. It is true that the development of taste in the field of commercial art and the opportunities now offered to the industrial designer have been matched by the discovery of talents in the animated film and by the decision of Canadian newspapers and magazines to use local illustrators and cartoonists. But the artist must, in the main, still fend for himself; nor is his task rendered easier by the immense number of amateur painters who compete with him in the galleries, though he may console himself with the thought that genius will out.

The most original of those whose work can be broadly identified neither with the Canadian landscape school nor with the Montreal group still remains David Milne. He continues to explore, with growing simplification and with spare dabs of his sensitive brush, scenes in small towns near Toronto. Lately he has added an element of charming fantasy to his work; and his water-colours have become freer and more fluid. He has the spirit of true discovery and though now approaching his later sixties, continues to be one of our great experimental painters.

Pegi Nicol Macleod, whose brilliant, if uneven career was cut short by her untimely death in 1949, developed an art which was at once so personal as to defy conventional analysis, and so vivid as to compel the attention of audiences both simple and sophisticated. Her bubbling enthusiasm, expressing itself in an unregulated and at times undisciplined flow, covered her canvases with a brilliant and cascading profusion of figures: children at play, sailors in a park, or nuns on a quiet, tree-lined street. The paintings are full of a lust for life, and the subject is seen so piercingly that sometimes the artist gives the impression of looking at the world without eyelids.

Paraskeva Clark's art is more formal and considered. Coming to Canada as a mature woman, she applied her Russian sense of explosive colour and her French love for classical form to the re-discovery of the Canadian landscape and people, with results that are at once joyous yet restrained, intense yet controlled. She is a naïve sophisticate with a beautifully grounded sense of composition and a rich understanding of tonal values.

To André Biéler belongs the discovery that the technique of the Group of Seven could be applied to humanistic portraiture and figure work; and that its bold planes and bright colours could be filtered through a veil of subtle underpainting which gave his pictures the luminous and lacquered patina of an old master. In his large mural for the Aluminum Company of Canada at Arvida, he succeeded, in a perhaps inimitable *tour de force,* in transferring this technique to painting on gesso backed by aluminum.

Jack Humphrey, working in solitary grandeur in New Brunswick, has distilled a personal and highly evocative mood, with a sense of transience and sadness. He has taken as his subject matter the tangle of red brick houses on the rocks of Saint John, his native city; the unexpected glimpse of receding planes across the harbour; and the tide nudging fishing boats higher in Market Slip. His painting is aloof, nostalgic and quietist.

In striking contrast to Humphrey, Henri Masson has surveyed the rolling sculptured forms of the Gatineau Hills near Ottawa, and has woven their bright colours into thinly painted, nervously incisive tapestries of light and line. His painting has immense vigour and his output is prolific. There is also a witty irony in his studies of children skating, of flooded householders at Gatineau Point, and in his many portraits of nuns, priests and friars in various attitudes of pious leisure and busy piety.

In Toronto a number of painters, owing much to the Group of Seven, has each made a personal contribution. Rody Courtice invests her still lifes and portraits with touches of whimsical originality; Yvonne McKague Housser and Isobel McLaughlin have each achieved a boldness and a well-controlled freedom in their landscapes and studies of trees and flowers. Peter Haworth remains one of our most solid water-colourists; and B. Cogill Haworth has brought to the study of boats, flowers and people a pleasing insouciance. Of interest also are the scraped and nervously energetic city scenes of William Winter, the more sophisticated studies of R. York Wilson, and the solidly painted compositions of John Alfsen and Leonard Brooks.

In yet another example of the richness of contemporary painting one finds Gordon Webber, a disciple of Moholy-Nagy, creating abstractions which have a real warmth and textural interest; while Edna Taçon, taking her cue from the freer abstractions of Klee and Kandinsky, creates canvases burnished with strange shapes whose freudian significance should probably not be insisted upon. The byzantine heads of John Hall, the acidly etched portraits of Maurice Reinblatt and the luscious paint of Mimi Parent and Simone Beaulieu are also notable.

On the West Coast a new star has arisen in that lively firmament. B. C. Binning, a draughtsman of exceptional skill and wit, first attracted notice by a series of complicated, yet disarmingly direct line drawings in both ink and pencil. They created mood, structure, social comment and a certain amount of quiet hilarity all in a single sinuous and calculated line. More recently his line has developed into subtle semi-abstract tonal relations, as in "Ships in a Calm".

Highly original also is Lillian Freiman, whose regrettably small output reveals a sureness of touch, a cogent sense of texture and an understanding of psychological values inferred through paint, that are rare in our art. She has sounded a single note, but has recently painted figure studies to equal her Breton work of almost twenty years ago. Her place is now with that of such younger masters of the craft as Jack Nichols and W. Roloff Beny.

In Vancouver, Jack Shadbolt has taken Emily Carr's vision of the rain forest, and has turned it into a savage indictment of the physical destruction of trees. Felled slash resembles torn limbs, and sheared stumps gape like wounds in the green depths. His older contemporary, J. W. G. MacDonald, still cleaves to the bright poster-like studies of landscapes and Indian villages which first brought him notice.[1]

In the realm of the graphic arts pride of place must go to Thoreau MacDonald for his magnificent book illustrations. These are instinct with the sombre breadth of great distances, and have a unique facility to render memorable such essentially Canadian themes as the low-topped Ontario

---

[1] Rising Western painters also include Maxwell Bates, Bill Calder, Don Jarvis and Bill Perehudoff.

hill, the curve of a northern river idling through the tundra, the wake of a canoe or the flight of a wedge of geese. He is ably companioned by Laurence Hyde, the exquisite craftsmanship of whose wood-engravings have adorned all too few of our publications; and by Grant Macdonald, whose notable portrait studies in line and wash show a genuine flair for character. Distinction in the graphic arts also continues to be gained by such older practitioners as Nicholas Hornyansky, W. J. Phillips, Leonard Hutchinson and Eric Bergman.

The general impression one receives from a survey of the contemporary field is that our artists need do no more than stop worrying about creating Canadian art, since this is precisely what they are doing in ever greater numbers. What is perhaps more important, they are creating with greater discrimination, with honest craftsmanship, and here and there with genuine inspiration and insight.

CHAPTER XII

Developments in Sculpture

SINCE THE DECLINE of the great Quebec school of ecclesiastical woodcarving, Canadian sculpture has laboured under two distinct disadvantages. During the period from about 1850 to the end of the First World War it fell victim to most of the ills common to late Victorian public statuary: dullness, pomposity and slavish naturalism. During the past thirty years it has had to struggle against the tendencies to rootlessness inherent in the so-called international style, and against the apathy of a public interested almost exclusively in painting.

In the high noon of the French-Canadian school, sculpture was the most notable art form produced. In one sense it remained so for some time; for though the tradition received a staggering blow with the delayed advent in Quebec of the industrial revolution, it survived in isolated cases for several decades. But these were exceptions; the driving force was spent, and while we may fancifully ascribe later Quebec sculpture to the influence of the Cap Tourmente tradition, it is plain that the inspiration was gone.

From the decline of French-Canadian woodcarving up to the formation of the Sculptors' Society of Canada in 1932, the art had no real institutional basis; and its exponents were few and far between, save in Quebec where, between 1875 and 1930, there was an era of public monuments. But there was nothing specifically native either in approach or technique: it naturally took longer for a more expensive and intractable medium to catch the spirit which had come over Canadian painting during the years 1912-1933. Shortly after the First World War sculptors drew together, students grew in numbers, and there was an aroused public interest in the craft, quickened, it must be admitted, by the necessity for the erection of war memorials.

Prior to this, most sculptors of note worked in the Province of Quebec. Chief among them was Philippe Hébert (1850-1917) whose work decorates many public buildings and may be seen in certain bronze memorials throughout the province and at Ottawa. Here the fine native tradition found a worthy descendant, though for the linear dynamism of the woodcarvers, Hébert substituted a certain caution and an interest in rounded form, the result of Italian influence. His work has a stolid grandeur, especially notable in the Maisonneuve monument in Montreal and some of the statuary decorating the Palais Legislatif at Quebec City.

Suzor-Côté, whose part in introducing Impressionism has already been discussed, also executed a number of bronze figurines, pleasantly conceived and, like his painting, impressionist in manner. In a group such as "Caughnawaga Women", a rhythmic study of Indian life, he achieved a majestic stature in little. Alfred Laliberté also executed genre pieces, some of which can be seen in the Musée Provincial at Quebec City. He was more prolific than Suzor-Côté, but lacked his sensitiveness; there appears a slight coarsening of the aesthetic fibre.

Bridging the gap between these men and a younger group of sculptors and their followers, stands Walter Allward, who by the sheer monumentality of his work, ranks high in the achievement of Canadian sculpture. Allward has been an eclectic, borrowing freely from all sources; but his own broadness of vision has enabled him to preserve his integrity. While his work sometimes seems to lack deep imaginative purpose, it has great breadth. This is seen at its best in the Bell memorial at Brantford, Ontario, and in the architectonic masses of the Canadian War Memorial at Vimy Ridge, where can be felt a sincerity and an understanding of the relation of mass to mass, which command respect.

The spirit of the Group of Seven found a strong echo, not only in outlook, but in subject matter, in a group of sculptors the most important of whom are Emanuel Hahn, Frances Loring and Florence Wyle. Emanuel Hahn, one of our finest craftsmen, has made a notable contribution to Canadian sculpture. In his work he has shown a vigorous understanding of plane relationships, as in his head of the explorer Vilhjalmur Stefansson; and an appreciation of mass and rhythm, as in his memorial to Sir Adam Beck, the founder of publicly owned hydro-electric power in Ontario. Whether in public monuments, portraiture or the design of coins, his work has always been distinguished by a strong sense of craft. Equally important has been his influence as a teacher and as an apologist for the art of sculpture. It was largely due to his initiative that the Sculptors' Society was formed.

The paths of Frances Loring and Florence Wyle have diverged from that of Hahn. Miss Loring has tended, on the whole, to produce work of powerful intensity with a strong linear flow. Her heroic lion at the entrance to the Queen Elizabeth Way near Toronto combines this flow with a strong feeling for mass and relation to the architectural background. Miss Wyle exhibits a flair for vigorous formal relationships, and has produced torsos and heads of a sinewy and satisfying strength.

Their work leads naturally to that of the younger artists, the most interesting of whom is Elizabeth Wyn Wood, who at one period achieved for sculpture what the Group of Seven achieved for painting. She took essentially Canadian subject matter, such as rocks, pines and even lakes, and successfully reproduced their direct spatial relationships. Working in tin, aluminum and glass her problems were naturally different from those of the painters, but she achieved results of equally startling originality. In her northern studies, she tended to ignore the volume and the planes of the medium in which she worked, and created airy, rhythmic pieces which are as passionately native as her colleagues' flowing, brightly coloured canvases. In other fields she has shown herself sensitive to plane, mass and volume, as in her figure work and even in her bas reliefs. She is one of the most original and thoughtful of our sculptors, and whether in the subdued and dignified pathos of her War Memorial at Welland, Ontario, or in the inspiration which she has given to her students, her contribution has been both powerful and constructive.

In Quebec, Sylvia d'Aoust and Ernst Neumann have both created heads and figures of considerable strength and delicacy; while Henri Hébert has successfully linked sculpture in low relief to architectural lines. Fine work has been done by Jacobine Jones, a craftsman of pronounced technical skill, and with a feeling for the relationship between sculpture and architectural mass. Alvin Hiltz has produced at Newmarket, Ontario, a war memorial of considerable power; Stephen Trenka has created carvings in wood of a wiry delicacy; the large nudes and heads of Orson Wheeler have a satisfying firmness; and in the firmly realized character studies of Byllee Lang, there is both a simple and a massive nobility.

The erection, during and after the Second World War, of a large number of public buildings, created a fresh opportunity for the use of sculpture. Though the results were

95

not uniformly good, they served to bring the art to the public notice. But those who commission public sculpture have not always understood its purpose; while the pages of the *Journal of the Royal Architectural Institute of Canada* have contained interesting debates between sculptors and architects as to where the responsibility lies for ensuring that sculpture is properly integrated with the mass of a building. Some examples of this apparent confusion may be pertinent.

Charles Comfort, whose superb murals in the Hotel Vancouver command high admiration, was forced, when he undertook to decorate the interior of the new Central Station of the Canadian National Railways in Montreal, to pour his talent into the procrustean bed of a machine-rendered bas relief. In the sculpture for the Bank of Montreal building in Toronto, sculptors were generously employed and work was commissioned from Emanuel Hahn, Donald Stewart, Jacobine Jones, Frances Loring, Florence Wyle and Elizabeth Wyn Wood. The sculpture was strong and formally well realized, but its relation to the mass of the building and to the view of the passer-by are still subjects of controversy in art circles. On the other hand, decorative designs by Jacobine Jones for the York Township building, Ontario, stood out well in stone against a brick background and seem to have secured more general approval.

In the winter of 1949-1950 the Sculptors' Society held a large exhibition, the first for many years; and it was possible to assess the value of the work being done. Such exhibitions reveal that the senior sculptors can, in general, still outpace their junior contemporaries; on the other hand, a number of the younger artists now produce very satisfying work. The fine, flowing, impressionistic heads of Cleeve Horne strengthen his position as one of our most successful exponents of the art of portrait sculpture. The work of Armand Filion shows a noble austerity. Donald Stewart's forceful figure work and the vivid bronzes of Sybil Kennedy also command a searching second look. But the influence of the international school is confined largely to the work of Louis Archambault and E. B. Cox, whose smoothly carved abstract shapes in various woods and stone, show a cunning appreciation of both texture and form.

In a smaller field, and in a lighter vein, Dora Wechsler continues to show her skill in the creation of ceramic figures satirizing social types; and these prove a welcome relief from those frightening torsos of women larger than life which are one of the more ponderous marks of contemporary sculpture.

The difficulty for sculptors in Canada has been that the immense cost, the massive weight and the intractable nature of their materials have made their products inaccessible to the average art lover save in miniature form. In a country whose population is as small as that of Canada, the sculptors' market will always be limited unless public buildings are made the occasion for public sculpture. The federal and provincial governments, which might be taking a lead in this matter, have so far been somewhat reluctant to do so. The lion at the entrance to the Queen Elizabeth Way is a welcome exception; so also are the striking murals designed by Eric Aldwinckle for the vast new veterans' hospital at Sunnybrook Park near Toronto, though here it is the painter rather than the sculptor who benefits. The New Post Office building, the Bank of Canada and the New Supreme Court building at Ottawa also bow to sculpture, but rather distantly.

As for public monuments, they have been, with very few exceptions, planned in the traditional late nineteenth-century manner: the conception is mortuary; the execution

pedestrian; and the statues usually placed on tall pedestals.
While this puts them well within the reach of birds, it
places them far beyond the gaze of ordinary mortals, who
usually obtain only a worm's-eye view of a frock coat or a
pair of gaiters.

The one great public monument commissioned by the
federal government in the past fifteen years, the National
War Memorial at Ottawa, must regrettably be accounted an
artistic failure. For every score of citizens or tourists who
gaze at its blindly representational figures and the symbolic
group above them, which appears to be in a permanent state
of deliquescence, there is perhaps one person who knows
that a fine example to all commissioners of war memorials
lies obscurely in a small park a mile to the south. This
is the bas relief of the Canadian Phalanx by the great
Yugoslav sculptor, Ivan Mestrovic. It is this deadening
homage to outworn tradition that makes so refreshing even
such comparatively orthodox ventures as Hahn's Beck Memorial or Elizabeth Wyn Wood's war memorial at Welland.

On the other hand, the appointment by the federal government, early in 1949, of the Royal Commission on National
Development in the Arts, Letters and Sciences, suggested
that a fresh approach might well be possible. If one adds
to architectural sculpture the generality of coins, bills and
stamps, there is every reason why this should be so. But
there is also reason to believe that the recommendations of
a body headed by so distinguished an art lover as Mr.
Massey may receive close attention, especially since the
National Capital Plan for the development of Ottawa calls
for the expenditure of public funds not only on landscaping
and railroad re-location, but also on public buildings.

CHAPTER XIII

The Allied Arts

IT IS NOT the purpose of this chapter to undertake an exhaustive review of the various applied arts. Such a survey would be beyond the scope of this book; and might easily degenerate into a mere catalogue of names and institutions. But the development of the allied arts in Canada during the past decade makes necessary at least a brief summary of what has been accomplished, together with some attempt to estimate the extent to which a Canadian style is beginning to emerge, and the level of public taste to be affected.

For a cumulative account of progress in the field of architecture, the reader is referred to the pages of that lively and distinctive publication, the *Journal of the Royal Architectural Institute of Canada,* and to the works cited in the bibliography at the end of this book. However, some brief notes may be appropriate. There has been an unprecedented volume of construction, both commercial and domestic, during the past decade; but despite suggestions to the contrary, it does not yet seem as if a recognizable Canadian style has been developed. It is true that any photograph of a Canadian city will at once proclaim its paternity; but this is due to eclectic borrowing, rather than to the emergence of a particular style.

Our new schools, office buildings and factories are modern international, and will be found to differ very little from their counterparts in the United States or Western Europe. The best of them, especially the multi-room one-storey schools, challenge comparison with the finest contemporary work. What is perhaps apparent to an outsider is that Canada is noticeably—and perhaps naturally, because of its immense forest resources—a country of wooden buildings. In general, these appear to have been flung down indiscriminately in accordance with immediate and urgent need, or with the desires of the speculative builder; so that the outstanding characteristic of a Canadian city is its untidiness and its appearance of temporariness. This has been enhanced in the post-war years by the erection of an immense number of small box-like houses on the fringes of every large city and town.

Most Canadian cities will show a small, almost obliterated core of early nineteenth-century stone and brick buildings of a vaguely Georgian cast, or, in the case of Quebec, St. Lawrence-Norman style. These will in turn be surrounded by a heavy layer of late nineteenth- and early twentieth-century buildings showing the influence of the Gothic revival. This influence is particularly evident in the case of legislative buildings, city halls, police stations, fire-halls and jails, and also in the existence of a large number of private mansions now cut up into flats and duplexes.

The larger cities will have their vertical thrust of sky-scrapers, the lines of those built later growing progressively simpler; or else the lateral thrust of "functional" office buildings, factories and schools, with their large areas of cement, glass brick, cantilevered canopies and generous window space. Beyond these fan out the suburban developments of wood, stucco and brick veneer: the older with heavy gables, towers, wooden filagree work and windows shaped like keys and horseshoes; the younger showing an extraordinary mixture of mock-Tudor, Georgian-surburban, girder-Gothic, Cape Cod Colonial or "moderne". Most of these are derivative or pastiche. Above them all rears the pseudo-Norman château of the railway hotel, transplanted from the Loire via Cass Gilbert and the steel frame. The whole is knit together with a tangle of overhead wires suspended from the gnarled and twisted cedar poles which still give Canadian cities their frontier appearance.

Planning is now very much in the air, and every city of any pretensions has its plan; but the costs involved necessarily make progress a long-term affair. In the meantime we may observe certain definite Canadian architectural expressions and may list certain buildings of distinction in the international style. Of the genuinely native developments may be mentioned the adaptation, in Quebec, to the uses of domestic architecture and the Laurentian ski resort, of the old country house noted in an earlier chapter. The giant terminal grain elevators at the head of Lake Superior, and at certain key points along the Great Lakes-St. Lawrence Waterway, are also a local form. The Ontario hipped barn, though duplicated in the Middle West, has a distinct native flavour; and the railway hotel, whatever its origins, carries definitely Canadian overtones. Of the government buildings on Parliament Hill in Ottawa it may be said that their site, combined with a free interpretation and mingling of the Gothic and château styles, has resulted in a perhaps considered unity, but also in an adventitious dignity and grandeur.

The modern buildings listed below do not constitute by any means an exhaustive list, but are typical of the best erected during the past decade. In Toronto: the Bank of Montreal Building, the plant of the Maclean-Hunter Publishing Company, Sunnybrook Hospital, the Bay-Wellington Building, the Bank of Nova Scotia Building, the Mechanical Building of the University of Toronto, and the Sales and Engineering Building of the Massey-Harris Company. In Montreal: the Central Station of the Canadian National Railways and its complex of related skyscrapers, the Imperial Oil Building, and the offices of the Shawinigan Water and Power Company. Among community projects may be noted the Victoria General Hospital, Halifax; the library, auditorium and art museum, London, Ontario; and the Pontiac Community Hospital, Shawville, P.Q. Among many notable factory buildings may be cited the plant of the Ontario Paper Company, Thorold, Ontario, and that of the Canadian Nashua Paper Company, Peterborough, Ontario. The immense size and massive majesty of the Shipshaw dam and power development near Arvida, Quebec, put it in a class of its own. The re-decoration of store fronts has proceeded apace since the war, with especially happy examples on the Pacific Coast; while new motion picture theatres of pleasing and dynamic line have been erected in a number of cities in Eastern Canada.

Where the Canadian designer has been guided by the combined considerations of function and appearance, definite progress has been made; and in the field of industrial design there have been marked achievements. The National Industrial Design Committee, under the chairmanship of Donald B. Cruickshank of Ottawa, and with Donald W. Buchanan as secretary, was formed in 1948. Its purpose is to promote a greater use of Canadian talent in the design of all types of consumer goods. The Committee is composed of some thirty manufacturers, retailers, designers, research and educational officials, and has associated with it certain members of government agencies interested in design. It received an initial grant from the federal government to cover organizational expenses, on the assumption that supplementary funds would later be obtained from industry in general.

The Committee seeks to bring to both manufacturers and consumers complete information about contemporary developments in industrial design. It has awarded to graduates of Canadian schools of engineering and architecture a number of post-graduate scholarships in industrial design, provided through the Board of Trustees of the National Gallery of Canada. The Committee undertakes detailed surveys of existing design facilities, and of present needs for trained designers in selected branches of Canadian manufacturing. An industrial design office, set up by the National Gallery in co-operation with the Committee, has established the Canadian Design Index, organized a library on product design, sponsored travelling exhibitions and displays, and distributed information and publications on industrial design.

Parallel with the foundation of the Committee, the Association of Canadian Industrial Designers was formed in 1948 to foster a high standard of design in industrial products as a service to the public, to industry and to "the national culture and economy". It also provides a legally constituted body which can establish standards of professional practice in industrial design, and which can advise on the practice and training of industrial designers in Canada.

The new interest shown in good design by businessmen and industrial firms is, of course, directly connected with Canada's need to compete in world export markets; and the indications are that our designers are not lagging behind their competitors in this field. Whether it be ranges or dining-cars, chairs or electric fans, they have shown themselves well able to adapt the international functional style to their own needs. In the process, they have purged it of some of the aridity which results from too slavish an adherence to the belief that function alone determines form.

In the allied field of typography, great strides have been taken. Canada has not yet designed, and perhaps does not need to design, type-fonts reflecting its own spirit. But the boom in the publishing of French language books in Montreal during the Second World War, and the close attention paid by certain advertising houses and national magazines to good type as a corollary to good lay-out, have resulted in a higher level of public demand for smooth, uncluttered and tasteful presentation. A number of firms, of which one of the most notable is that of Crossman-Eveleigh-Dair in Montreal, have in turn made it their business to educate the advertisers.

Advertising nevertheless remains, as it must, heavily influenced by the current naturalistic styles of American houses, among which such skilled and original men as Paul Rand and Jean Carlu remain in a small minority. The plunge into abstraction or surrealism is generally taken only by those houses and magazines which advertise women's clothing. In the attempts to break away from the materialistic influence, the work of Clair Stewart and Alan Harrison must be accounted successful. The use of Canadian paintings by such firms as Imperial Oil Limited, the Canadian Pulp and Paper Association and Canada Packers Limited is also worth noting.

Display and exhibition have markedly improved during the past ten years, and there is a definite interest today in display techniques as such. Leadership in this field has fallen to the re-organized Canadian Government Exhibition Commission under the direction of Glen Bannerman, with Tom Wood as chief designer; and to certain commercial firms, notably Canadian Industries Limited. Even so large and popular a public festival as the annual Canadian National Exhibition in Toronto will present, in a normal year, several displays well above the average; while the mounting of the Canadian International Trade Fair has been a credit to all concerned.

The growth of the Little Theatre movement and the establishment of a professional theatre in Montreal, Toronto and Ottawa, has given Canadian artists and designers a chance to try their hand at stage sets. Further impetus has been given to their efforts by the work of local playwrights; and talented stage designers have been discovered in Alfred Pellan and Robert La Palme, who did the sets for Gratien Gélinas' ("Fridolin") revue "Tit-coq", and Grant Macdonald, who performed a similar service for Robertson Davies' "Fortune, my Foe". The move to establish a Canadian ballet has also given opportunities for *décor* and costume of which advantage is sure to be taken.

One of the most stimulating events of the past decade has been the opening up of the medium of the film to artists, cartoonists and animators. The initiative taken by the National Film Board in this respect has been followed by commercial film producers. In a field which contains much interesting work, leadership undoubtedly falls to Norman Maclaren whose drawings, direct on film, have produced a unique art form which has caught the attention of such a majestic figure as Picasso. Others whose animation is highly talented include Jean-Paul Ladouceur, James Mackay, Guy Glover, George Dunning and Graham Crabtree. The work of the two former artists in the National Film Board's series of animated French-Canadian folk songs, "Chants Populaires", has been one of the liveliest developments of the past few years.

Cartooning and caricature for the daily and periodical press has also assumed a fresh interest. Newspapers now take renewed pride in their own cartoonists; and apart from La Palme, who is inimitable, mention should be made of John Collins of the Montreal *Gazette,* Reidford of the *Montreal Daily Star*; Chambers of the *Halifax Chronicle-Herald*; Grassick and Simpkins of *Maclean's Magazine*; and the free-lance illustrators and cartoonists Peter Whalley, Franklin Arbuckle, Harold Towne and Oscar Cahen. The prestige which the work of such skilled illustrators has given to our national press is as encouraging as the foresight of the editors who have employed them. To anyone comparing the journals of 1940 with those of 1950 the change in presentation is particularly startling. One feels that the distance between them is closer to a generation than to a decade.

In the ceramic arts, Kjeld and Erica Deichmann continue to hold their lead in a profession which is becoming well established in both output and quality. The skilled metal work of such artists as Harold Stacey and V. Shabaeff is giving distinction to this exacting craft. These men are professionals; but the whole field of handicrafts has been actively stimulated by the work of the Canadian Handicrafts Guild, and, more particularly in Quebec, by the provincially sponsored Ecole du Meuble. Those who see in such work merely a desire to perpetuate the vanished skills that created the *ceinture fléchée,* the hooked rug, or the pious woodcarving for the mantel, miss the point. These skills have their roots deep in our past and our nature; and their adaptation to modern needs is a confession of strength rather than of escapist weakness.

It is true that the great majority of our artifacts still show the mark of the machine, and a coarseness of taste which only a fanatical patriot would suggest was due solely, or even partially, to the necessity for pleasing tourists from the south. A visit to the "art" section of a city store can be a most depressing experience, beginning with the contorted and derivative signs which all too frequently invite one to enter. But in these matters, time must take its course, and no one will gainsay that its course, during the past decade, has been a rapid one.

CHAPTER XIV

Art and the Public

UNQUESTIONABLY PUBLIC INTEREST in the visual arts now stands at a very much higher level than ever before in our history. It is equally certain, however, that it has still not become part of the warp and woof of our national life, as it is in many European and Latin American countries. It may be doubted whether it ever will become so. Though the tendency to sneer at philistia has been tempered by the realization that the world of the philistines was at least stable and predictable, there remain with us too much both of newness and of Anglo-Saxon folkways for this country ever to breathe in art through its pores in the manner of an older civilization. But if one compares the present, not with what might be, but with what was, one notes remarkable changes.

Canada now has a magazine devoted exclusively to comment on the visual arts; and art criticism is undertaken seriously by a number of national periodicals and metropolitan dailies. Though criticism in the smaller centres often fails to distinguish amateur from professional (the standard is aesthetic, not monetary) and accords all comers equal treatment, this is something that time will cure. And while the work of the Sunday painter should not seriously be considered in any assessment of our national art, it has an undoubted virtue from the standpoint of individual happiness and leisure employment, and of useful community activity.

There has been a notable growth in the influence of art galleries through extra-mural work. A number of these institutions, such as the National Gallery of Canada, the Musée Provincial in Quebec City, the Montreal Museum of Fine Arts, the Art Gallery of Toronto, the Royal Ontario Museum and the Vancouver Art Gallery, have distinguished collections, and play an important part in art education and extension work in their own communities. Many galleries and museums have joined forces in the Canadian Museums Association, which holds annual conventions where professional problems are discussed.

For Canadian painting, though not as yet for sculpture, there is now a reasonably sure market; and prices have reached the level at which the artist is assured of a return for his labours, while the private collector does not find the cost beyond his reach. The artists themselves have formed an organization to act as their collective spokesman and to further their common aims. The Federation of Canadian Artists was formed in 1941 as the result of a meeting at Queen's University, Kingston, Ontario, sponsored by the National Gallery. The Federation can deal with artists' problems, care for their interests and, on occasion, present briefs to appropriate bodies.

The adult education movement, greatly stimulated by the rehabilitation programmes immediately after the Second World War, has found a ready response to art work in community centres. Films produced by the National Film Board on Canadian artists and their work have also been distributed free on the Board's rural circuits. In the field of radio, the co-operative venture of the Canadian Broadcasting Corporation and the National Gallery in bringing art appreciation courses to schools reflects great credit on both bodies, and especially on Richard S. Lambert, the CBC's director of educational broadcasts. Silk screen reproductions of Canadian paintings were circulated widely during the Second World War, under the sponsorship of the

National Gallery, the armed forces, and the Canadian Legion Educational Services. They filled the walls of many training camps, barracks, messes and factories, and there is no doubt that their presence resulted in a much wider public familiarity with contemporary painting.

The formation, in 1945, of the Canadian Arts Council, has tended to give artists a corporate status commensurate with the public interest now accorded to their profession. It has also enabled them to secure a hearing in official circles. With the establishment, in 1945, of the United Nations Educational, Scientific and Cultural Organization, the opportunities for artists to express, as a body, their views in the international field, were considerably increased. Canada is a member of UNESCO, and Canadian delegations to its conferences have included members of both the Federation of Canadian Artists and the Canadian Arts Council.

Since the war Canadian painters have also had an increased opportunity to exhibit their works abroad. The National Gallery, often in co-operation with the Department of External Affairs, has arranged a number of major exhibitions on the basis of which critical comment has indicated that our art, judged by international standards, has been found varied and stimulating. In addition to the exhibitions held in Brazil, mentioned in an earlier chapter, major showings have been held in recent years in Buenos Aires, Santiago, the cities of New Zealand, Rome, Paris, and in a number of United States centres, including New Haven, Albany, Cleveland, Detroit, New York, Richmond, and Boston.

Reference has been made in an earlier chapter to the establishment, by the federal government, of the Royal Commission on National Development in the Arts, Letters and Sciences.

109

In a film made some years ago by the National Film Board, A. Y. Jackson uttered a penetrating comment concerning the artist's search for realization. "Anything you need, you will find", said Jackson, "but you must sense the need of it". This little apophthegm is as valid for the public as for the artists; and indeed failure to sense the need for the place of art in our national life is now the only factor which could prevent its achieving its rightful position. For the artists are here, and to the acclaim achieved in their own country has now been added that of their admirers abroad. It remains only to achieve, in the classic Canadian manner, a compromise between those who favour some form of centralized aid, and those who are content that artist and public should be brought together through a recognition of their common interest in and need for each other. There is every evidence that this recognition, accelerated by the stormy events of the past ten years, is now being achieved.

CHAPTER XV

A National Art?

T HIS BOOK BEGAN by stating the problem that has faced artists in all new countries: whether to strive consciously for a native expression; or whether to create as one feels, and thereby naturally achieve an art which will be recognizably regional. These attitudes ebb and flow throughout the more recent history of art in Canada, as they do in Australia or the United States. To the woodcarver of New France, no such problem was presented; nor to the designer of the canoe or the snowshoe. All three created works which are at once superbly designed and indubitably Canadian. But in our own time the position has been complicated by a conscious awareness of certain social and political factors.

Inevitably, the development of art in Canada has been interwoven with our struggle to achieve nationhood. The psychological attitude of Canada toward both the United Kingdom and the United States has been shown in two diverse but equally revealing ways: the tendency toward slavish imitation of what are regarded as the distant, and therefore greater glories of older lands; and the brash assumption of independence with its conscious search for a native expression, and its deliberate bursting of old bonds.

The industrial revolution and the general breakdown of the comfortable and seemingly inevitable pattern of nineteenth-century life, brought to Canada the influence of the so-called international style. During the past forty years the air has been rent with the cries of those who wished, on the one hand, to be Canadian, and those who wished, on

111

the other hand, to be sophisticated. Yet such is the influence of environment that those who desired to be passionately Canadian, and those who desired simply to produce the vision that was in them have both ended by creating a vigorous national art.

We are a sober people, greatly given to worrying about our own problems. It has been said that if three of us assemble in a room, the conversation will turn, sooner or later, to the Great Canadian Problems: how we are to reconcile the points of view of French- and English-speaking Canada, of East and West, of Anglophil and Americanophil, of nationalist and traditionalist. Yet before the immutable and ever-present facts of our harsh and timeless background, we are at one: silent, aware, and deeply, though not ostentatiously moved. And it is the background which, whether we will it or not, and despite any conscious effort on our part to quicken the pace of our development, will determine what we are.

We live in an era of transition, and in a country that is in a hurry. The temptation to create, overnight, conditions in which we can produce an art that will reflect what we conceive to be our nature, is overwhelming. But the important thing is that in a century of struggle and of sporadic creative endeavour, we have finished by producing an art that is both recognizably Canadian, and capable of being judged by international standards.

Should this concern us? Ultimately, not only art, but the social pattern which produces it, are the reflection of environment; and Canada is above all a land where, before nature—endless, massive and uncaring—our artists have a sense of brooding, or of violent unease. We are all subconsciously aware of the inexorable mass of our land, and of the constant pressure of natural forces which, with all our technical achievement, we shall never wholly subdue

112

and have succeeded only in holding at bay. Canada is an act of faith, and its mere existence often a cause of admiration and wonder. Beyond the narrow fringe of a civilized and technically developed community, looms the Shield; and with it, the barrens, the "North Country", the canoe, and that hostage to the Pre-Cambrian—the summer cottage. We are not Latins and do not react as such. We are not addicted to dancing and light wines, but to hockey and rye whisky. Like most northern peoples, our art and our music have uttered the same notes of protest and resignation. Like most peoples familiar with vast spaces and a vigorous climate, our creative expression has been in turn both contemplative and violent.

Immense distances and bare rock compel us to spend a huge proportion of our national effort and income on the mere essential services designed to keep the country going. No Canadian who has felt the winter sky creak, and a howling wind from the Arctic send the mercury tumbling down far below zero, ever feels, even in an office building, that he is completely master of the elements. No Canadian who has driven north from the main Montreal-Quebec highway, and within ten miles has found three-hundred-year-old farms petering out against the shoulders of the Laurentians, can ever feel completely sure of himself. This stark brute force, which has terrified and inspired our poets, novelists and painters alike, has induced in us a sense of sombre pride. The elements will determine what we are; and they are so vast and incalculable that we who live in the narrow fringe will react, in our art, in protest, in resignation, in sudden wonder; but rarely with suavity, delicacy or charm.

This, then, is our art. It is a reflection of a modern, complex, technical society, superimposed upon an elemental land. That we love this land deeply does not make it love

113

us; and we scurry back to our cabins when the wind blows keen. Yet at the same time, we dare it to blow on us more fiercely. Blake remarks that great things are done when men and mountains meet. In Canada, men and mountains are meeting every day; and out of that meeting has come an art compounded of technical sophistication and brute force; of wonder, and violence and joy. It is a vital and vivid art; but it is not at ease with itself. Nor should it ever be so. Our polemicists and critics may urge us on to the creation of a National Art; but what we are getting is a national art—lower case, please—that is a true reflection of our vast, unsentimental land.

Select list of Art Institutions and Public Art Collections.

For a fuller list of Art Institutions and public collections see *Directory of Museums and Art Galleries in Canada, etc.,* compiled by Sir Henry A. Miers and S. F. Markham, and published by the Museums Association.

BRITISH COLUMBIA
    Victoria: The Provincial Museum. Indian Art.
    Vancouver: The Vancouver Art Gallery. English and Canadian paintings and sculpture.

ALBERTA
    Calgary: The Calgary Allied Arts Council, the Coste House.
    Edmonton: The Edmonton Museum of Arts. Canadian painting.

SASKATCHEWAN
    Regina: The Mackenzie Foundation, Regina College. Italian Renaissance, English, French, Dutch, German and Canadian painting.
    Saskatoon: The Saskatoon Art Centre.

MANITOBA
    Winnipeg: The Winnipeg Art Gallery. English and Canadian painting.
    The Winnipeg Museum. Indian Art.
    The Museum of the Hudson's Bay Company. Historical exhibits.

ONTARIO
    Hamilton: The Art Gallery of Hamilton. Canadian painting and Canadiana.
    London: The London Public Library and Art Museum. Canadian painting and sculpture, and Canadiana.
    Ottawa: The National Gallery of Canada. Italian (especially Venetian), French, Spanish, Dutch, Flemish, German, English and Canadian painting. Canadian and other sculpture. Prints.
    The National Museum of Canada. Indian Art.
    The Public Archives. Canadian paintings and topographical work.

Toronto: The Art Gallery of Toronto. English, French, Flemish, German and Canadian painting. Canadian and other sculpture.

The Royal Ontario Museum. Chinese (one of the finest on the continent), Japanese, Near Eastern, Italian, French, English, Greek, Roman, Etruscan and Egyptian Art. Canadian handicrafts.

The John Ross Robertson Collection of the Toronto Public Libraries. Canadiana.

QUEBEC

Montreal: The Montreal Museum of Fine Arts. French, English, Dutch, Italian and Canadian painting. Sculpture and applied arts.

The Château de Ramezay. Historical exhibits.

The McCord Museum, McGill University. Canadiana.

Quebec City: Musée Provincial. Canadian painting and sculpture. Canadiana.

Laval University Collection. Italian and Spanish painting. Canadian carving, etc.

Murray Bay: Manoir Richelieu Collection. Topographical art, prints and Canadiana.

NOVA SCOTIA

Halifax: The Provincial Archives. Canadiana.

Annapolis: The Fort Anne Historical Museum. Canadiana.

NEW BRUNSWICK

Saint John: The New Brunswick Museum. Chinese and Near Eastern art. The J. Clarence Webster Collection of Canadiana.

PRINCE EDWARD ISLAND

Charlottetown: The Harris Memorial Gallery. Work of Robert Harris.

Chronology

1534	Cartier in the St. Lawrence.
1604	De Monts founds Port Royal (later Annapolis).
1608	Champlain founds Quebec.
1675	Mgr. Laval establishes his Ecole des Arts et Métiers.
1678	Père Hennepin at Niagara Falls. First topographical view.
1685-6	Deaths of Frères Luc and Pommier.
1671-92	Construction of the Hôpital Général, Quebec.
1704	Construction of the Château de Ramezay, Montreal.
c 1710-75	The Levasseurs at work in Quebec.
1741-1850	The Baillairgés at work in Quebec.
1742-9	Construction of the Church of Ste. Famille, Ile d'Orléans.
1750 on	The Labrosses at work in Montreal.
1759	Fall of Quebec.
1776	The American Revolution breaks out.
1780	Death of Abbé J-A Aide Créquy, first native-born painter.
1780-1812	Influx of United Empire Loyalists.
1802-20	Quevillon School active at Montreal.
1812-14	War against the United States.
1823	Death of Louis Quevillon.
1834	Formation of the Society of Artists and Amateurs of Toronto.
1837	Rebellions in Upper and Lower Canada.
1842	Publication of Bartlett's *Canadian Scenery*.
1847	Formation of the Toronto Society of Artists.
1859	Publication of Kane's *Wanderings of an Artist*. Death of Thomas Baillairgé.
1860	Foundation of the Art Association of Montreal.
1867	Confederation. Formation of the Canadian Society of Artists.
1871	Death of Paul Kane.
1872	Death of Cornelius Krieghoff. Formation of the Ontario Society of Artists.
1873-94	*Grip* published.
1875	Foundation of the school which in 1912 became the Ontario College of Art.
1880	Foundation of the National Gallery of Canada. Formation of the Royal Canadian Academy.
1885	First transcontinental train.

1886	Hodgson's report.
	Art Students' League founded in Toronto.
1890	Foundation of Owens Art Gallery, Mount Allison University, Sackville, N.B.
	Foundation of Women's Art Association.
1893-1903	Art Students' League Calendar.
1896-1908	Quebec Students' Club.
1900	Art Museum (Art Gallery) of Toronto incorporated.
1905	Foundation of Canadian Society of Graphic Art.
1906	Gallery erected at Canadian National Exhibition.
1907	Formation of Canadian Art Club.
	Advisory Arts Council of National Gallery.
1912	Formation of the Montreal Arts Club.
	Foundation of the Royal Ontario Museum.
1913	First *Yearbook of the Arts* published.
	Trustees appointed to the National Gallery.
1914	Studio Building completed at Toronto.
	Outbreak of the First World War.
1914-15	Travelling Patriotic Exhibition.
1916	"The Tangled Garden" exhibited.
1917	Death of Thomson.
1919	War Memorials completed.
	Formation of Society of Canadian Painter-Etchers and Engravers.
1920	Formation of Group of Seven.
1924	Death of Morrice.
1924-5	Wembley Exhibitions of Canadian painting.
1925	Formation of the Manitoba Society of Artists.
1926	Foundation of the Canadian Society of Painters in Water-Colour.
1927	Paris Exhibition of Canadian painting.
1928	Death of Louis Jobin
1931	Foundation of the Vancouver Art Gallery.
1932	Death of MacDonald.
	Miers-Markham report on Canadian museums.
	Reorganization of the New Brunswick Museum.
	Formation of the Sculptors' Society of Canada.
1933	Formation of the Canadian Group of Painters.
1934	Death of Cullen.
1935	Formation of the Maritime Art Association.
1936	Death of Watson.
1937	Coronation Exhibition in London, England.
1938	"A Century of Canadian Art" Exhibition in London, England.
	Death of Walker.
1939	Death of Eric Brown, first Director of the National Gallery of Canada.

118

Exhibitions of Canadian art at the New York World's Fair.

Outbreak of the Second World War.

1940 Foundation of the magazine *Maritime Art*.

First Guggenheim Fellowship awarded to a Canadian painter (Carl Schaefer).

1941 Meeting at Kingston to found the Federation of Canadian Artists.

1942 Canadian War Artists commissioned.

1943 Sicilian campaign.

Start of Italian campaign.

Foundation of the magazine *Canadian Art*.

1944 Normandy campaign.

Exhibitions of Canadian art in Brazil (winter 1944-45).

1945 End of Second World War.

Death of Emily Carr.

Foundation of Canadian Arts Council.

Foundation of Canadian Museums Association.

1946 First General Conference of UNESCO.

Second Guggenheim Fellowship awarded to a Canadian painter (Jack Nichols).

1947 Death of Prudence Heward.

1948 Foundation of the National Industrial Design Committee.

1949 Appointment of the Royal Commission on National Development in the Arts, Letters and Sciences.

Union of Newfoundland with Canada.

Death of Pegi Nicol Macleod.

1950 Fiftieth anniversary of the foundation of the Art Gallery of Toronto.

Select List of Canadian Artists

ABBREVIATIONS:
WC.—Woodcarver   Arch.—Architect
S. —Sculptor   G.   —Graphic Artist
T. —Topographer   C.   —Cartoonist

DECEASED

Ahrens, Carl	1863-1936
Atkinson, W. E.	1862-1926
Baillairgé, Jean WC	*c* 1741
Baillairgé, François WC	*b* 1759
Baillairgé, Florent WC	*b* 1761
Baillairgé, Thomas WC	1792-1859
Barnsley, J. M.	1861-1929
Bartlett, Capt. W. H. T	1809-1854
Beatty, J. W.	1869-1941
Beaucourt, F. M. de	1740-1794
Beaufoy, Capt. B. T	*fl* 1830
Bell-Smith, F. M.	1846-1923
Bengough, J. W. C	1851-1923
Bennett, Major W. J. T	1787-1844
Berthon, G. T.	1806-1892
Brownell, Franklin	1856-1946
Bruce, Blair	1859-1906
Brymner, William	1855-1925
Carlyle, Florence	1864-1923
Carmichael, Franklin	1890-1945
Carr, Emily	1871-1945
Cockburn, Maj.-Gen. Sir J. T	1779-1847
Coke-Smyth T	*fl* 1842-1867
Côté, J-B. WC	1805-1870
Créquy, Abbé J-A. Aide	1749-1780
Cresswell, William	1822-1888
Cruikshank, William	1849-1922
Cullen, Maurice	1866-1934
David, Louis B. WC	*c* 1812
Davis, Major H. T	*c* 1818
Day, Forshaw	1837-1903
Downman, J. T. T.	1750-1824

120

Eager, William T	1796-1839
Eaton, Wyatt	1849-1896
Field, Robert	1767-1819
Fowler, Daniel	1819-1894
Fraser, J. A.	1838-1898
Gagen, Robert	1848-1926
Gagnon, Clarence	1881-1942
Gosselin, Gabriel WC	c 1795
Hamel, Eugène	1845-1932
Hammond, John	1843-1939
Hancock, J. T	c 1794
Harris, Robert	1849-1919
Hébert, Philippe S	1850-1917
Heming, Arthur	1870-1940
Hennepin, Père Louis T	1640-1710
Hennessy, Frank	1893-1941
Heriot, George T	1766-1844
Heward, Prudence	1896-1947
Holmes, Robert	1861-1930
Jobin, Louis WC	1843-1928
Jacobi, Otto	1812-1901
Johnston, Franz	1888-1948
Julien, Henri C	1851-1908
Kane, Paul	1810-1871
Knowles, F. McG.	1859-1932
Krieghoff, Cornelius	1815-1872
Labrosse, J. WC	c 1760
Leblond de Latour WC	c 1690
Levasseur, Jean WC	1717-1775
Levasseur, François WC	1703—?
Levasseur, Noël WC	1680-1740
Luc, Frère	d1685
McKenzie, Tait	1867-1938
MacDonald, J. E. H.	1873-1932
Macleod, Pegi Nicol	1904-1949
Manly, C. M.	1855-1924
Martin, T. M.	1838-1934
Morrice, J. W.	1865-1924
Morris, Edmund	1871-1913

121

Neilson, H. I. 1865-1931

O'Brien, L. R. 1832-1899

Paquet, André wc .... c 1838-44
Peachey, Lt. J. t .... c 1783-99
Peel, Paul 1860-1892
Plamondon, Antoine 1804-1895
Pommier, Frère H. .... c 1686

Quevillon, Louis wc 1749-1823
Quevillon School wc .... c 1802-20

Reid, G. A. 1860-1947
Robson, A. H. 1882-1939
Russell, G. H. 1861-1923

Sandham, J. H. 1842-1910
Short, Richard t .... c 1739-61
Simpson, C. W. 1878-1942
Suzor-Côté, M-A de F. 1869-1937

Thomson, Tom 1877-1917

Valentine, William 1798-1849
Verner, F. A. 1836-1928

Walker, Horatio 1858-1938
Warre, Capt. H. t 1819-1898
Watson, Homer 1855-1936
Williamson, Curtis 1867-1944

Contemporary

Aldwinckle, Eric 1909-
Alfred, Paul 1892-
Alfsen, John 1902-
Allward, Walter S. s 1876-
Arbuckle, Franklin 1909-
Atkins, Caven 1907-

Bates, Maxwell 1906-
Beament, Harold 1898-
Beny, W. Roloff 1924-
Bercovitch, Aleksandre 1893-
Bergman, Eric 1893-
Biéler, André 1897-
Binning, B. C. 1909-
Bonnycastle, Murray 1909-

Borduas, P-E 1905-
Borenstein, Samuel 1908-
Brandtner, Fritz 1896-
Brigden, Fred H. 1871-
Brittain, Miller 1914-
Brooker, Bertram 1888-
Brooks, Leonard 1911-

Cahen, Oscar c 1916-
Casson, A. J. 1898-
Challener, F. S. 1869-
Chicoine, René 1905-
Clark, Paraskeva 1898-
Coburn, F. S. 1871-
Collins, John c 1917-
Comfort, Charles F. 1900-
Cosgrove, Stanley 1912-
Courtice, Rody 1895-

Dair, Carl 1910-
Daly, Kathleen 1898-
d'Aoust, Sylvia s 1902-
des Clayes, Alice 1891-

Eveleigh, Henry 1909-

Farley, Lillias 1918-
Fisher, Orville 1911-
Fitzgerald, L. L. 1890-
Forbes, Kenneth 1892-
Forster, Michael 1907-
Fortin, Marc-Aurèle 1888-
Fosbery, Ernest 1874-
Freiman, Lillian 1908-
Fugler, Grace g 1915-

Gauthier, Joachim 1897-
Godfrey, W. F. G. g 1884-
Goldberg, Eric 1890-
Goldhamer, Charles 1903-
Grier, Sir Wyly 1862-

Hahn, Emanuel s 1881-
Haines, Fred S. 1879-
Hall, John 1916-
Harris, Lawren 1885-
Harris, Lawren, Jr. 1909-
Harrison, Alan 1911-
Haworth, Peter 1889-

Haworth, B. Cogill 1900-
Hébert, Adrien 1890-
Hébert, Henri s 1890-
Henderson, J. 1871-
Hewton, Randolph 1888-
Hiltz, Alvin s 1908-
Holgate, E. H. 1892-
Hornyansky, Nicholas 1896-
Housser, Yvonne McK. 1898-
Hughes, E. J. 1913-
Humphrey, Jack 1901-
Hutchinson, Leonard 1896-
Hyde, Laurence 1914-

Jackson, A. Y. 1882-
Jefferys, C. W. 1869-
Jones, Jacobine 1898-

Kerr, Estelle 1879-

Ladouceur, J-P c 1921-
Laliberté, Alfred s 1878-
Lang, Bylee 1908-
Lapine, André 1868-
Lawson, Ernest 1873-
Lemieux, J-P 1904-
Lismer, Arthur 1885-
Lockerby, Mabel 1887-
Long, Marion 1882-
Loring, Frances s 1887-
Lyman, John 1886-

MacDonald, A. A. 1909-
MacDonald, J. W. G. 1887-
Macdonald, Grant 1913-
MacDonald, Thoreau 1901-
McLaughlin, Isabel ....
Masson, Henri 1907-
May, Mabel 1884-
McKay, James c 1916-
McLaren, Norman 1914-
Milne, David B. 1884-
Morris, Kathleen 1898-
Muhlstock, Louis 1904-
Munn, Kathleen 1887-

Nelson, Helen s 1914-
Neumann, Ernst s 1907-

Newton, Lilias T. 1896-
Nichols, Jack 1921-

Ogilvie, Will A. 1901-

Palmer, H. S. 1881-
Panton, L. A. C. 1894-
Pellan, Alfred 1906-
Pepper, George 1903-
Phillips, W. J. 1884-

Reidford, W. G 1911-
Reinblatt, Maurice 1917-
Roberts, Goodridge 1904-
Robertson, Sarah 1891-
Robinson, A. H. 1881-
Ross, Robert G 1902-

Savage, Anne 1897-
Schaefer, Carl 1903-
Scott, C. H. 1886-
Scott, Marian 1906-
Seath, Ethel 1879-
Shadbolt, Jack 1909-
Shaw, Avery 1907-
Sheppard, Peter 1882-
Smith, Jori 1905-
Stevens, Dorothy 1888-
Stewart, Clair 1910-
Stewart, Donald 1912-
Surrey, Philip 1910-

Taçon, Edna 1913-
Thomson, George 1868-
Thorne, John G 1921-
Tonnancour, J. de 1917-
Towne, Harold 1924-
Trenka, Stephen 1908-

Varley, F. H. 1881-

Webber, Gordon 1909-
Weston, W. P. 1879-
Whalley, Peter G 1921-
Wheeler, Orson 1902-
Wherry, Sheila 1915-
Wood, E. Wyn 1903-
Wood, Tom 1913-
Wrinch, Mary 1877-
Wyle, Florence 1881-

Select Bibliography

This bibliography is divided into three sections: books; periodicals; films and filmstrips.

BOOKS

General

BUCHANAN, DONALD W., *Canadian Painters*. Phaidon Press, London, 1945

BUCHANAN, DONALD W., *The Growth of Canadian Painting*. Collins, Toronto, 1950

COLGATE, WILLIAM, *Canadian Art,* 1820-1940. Ryerson Press, Toronto, 1943

JEFFERYS, C. W., *The Picture Gallery of Canadian History*. Ryerson Press, Toronto, 1942

HAMMOND, M. O., *Painting and Sculpture in Canada*. Ryerson Press, Toronto, 1930

LAMBERT, R. S., *The Adventure of Canadian Painting*. McClelland & Stewart, Toronto, 1947. (For young people)

LISMER, ARTHUR, *A Short History of Painting*. Andrews, Toronto, 1926

LISMER, ARTHUR, *Education through Art*. Art Gallery of Toronto, Toronto, 1936

MASSEY, RT. HON. VINCENT, *Art and Nationality in Canada*. Trans. Royal Soc. of Canada, Ottawa, 1930

McRAE, D. G. W., *The Arts and Crafts of Canada*. Macmillan, Toronto, 1944

MIERS, SIR H. and MARKHAM, S. F., *Report on the Museums of Canada*. The Museums Assn., London, 1932

MORRIS, EDMUND, *Art in Canada*. General Publishing, Toronto, 1912

ROBSON, A. H., *Canadian Landscape Painters*. Ryerson Press, Toronto, 1932

American Art Annual. American Federation of Arts, Washington, 1948 (Lists Canadian art museums, societies and schools)

Art Gallery of Toronto. Catalogues and annual reports

Montreal Museum of Fine Arts. Catalogues and reports

Arts of French Canada. Institute of Arts, Detroit, 1946. Exhibition catalogue with text and illustrations

Development of Painting in Canada: Le Développement de la peinture au Canada. Ryerson Press, Toronto, 1945. Exhibition catalogue with text and illustrations.

National Gallery of Canada. Catalogue of Paintings (The Permanent Collection), Ottawa, 1948

National Gallery of Canada. Catalogues and annual reports

Ontario Society of Artists, Toronto. Catalogues from 1873 onwards

Royal Canadian Academy. Catalogues from 1882 onwards

Who's Who in American Art. American Federation of Arts, Washington, 1948. (Lists directory of Canadian artists)

Native Arts

BAILEY, A. G., *The Conflict of Cultures.* University of New Brunswick, Saint John, 1937

BARBEAU, MARIUS, *The Downfall of Temlaham.* Macmillan, Toronto, 1928

BARBEAU, MARIUS, *The Growth of the Totem Pole.* Smithsonian Reprint, Washington, 1940

BARBEAU, MARIUS, *The Totem Poles of the Gitksan.* Trans. Royal Soc. of Canada, Ottawa, 1929

BOAZ, FRANZ, *Primitive Art,* Harvard University Press, Cambridge, Mass., 1938

JENNESS, DIAMOND, *Eskimo Art.* American Geographical Society, New York, 1922

Quebec: The Great Tradition

BARBEAU, MARIUS, *Ceintures fléchées.* Editions Paysana, Montreal, 1946

BARBEAU, MARIUS, *Côté the Woodcarver.* Trans. Royal Soc. of Canada, Ottawa, 1943

BARBEAU, MARIUS, *Le dernier de nos grands artisans, Louis Jobin.* Trans. Royal Soc. of Canada, Ottawa, 1933

BARBEAU, MARIUS, *Maîtres artisans de chez nous.* Editions du Zodiaque, Montreal, 1942

BARBEAU, MARIUS, *Quebec où survit l'ancienne France.* Librairie Garneau, Quebec, 1937

BARBEAU, MARIUS, *Saintes artisanes.* 2 vols. Editions Fidès, Montreal, 1944-46

BARBEAU, MARIUS, *Two Centuries of Woodcarving in Canada.* Trans. Royal Soc. of Canada, Ottawa, 1933

MORISSET, GÉRARD, *Coup d'oeil sur les arts en Nouvelle France.* The Author, Quebec, 1941

MORISSET, GÉRARD, *François Ranvoysé.* The Author, Quebec, 1942

MORISSET, GÉRARD, *La vie et l'oeuvre du Frère Luc.* Quebec, 1944

ROY, P. G. (Ed.) *Bulletin des Recherches Historiques,* IV, 23; VI, 150; XXII, 3; XXV, 153

ROY, P. G. (Ed.) *Les Vieilles Eglises de la Province de Quebec.* Proulx, Quebec, 1925

Roy, P. G. *l'Ile d'Orléans.* Proulx, Quebec, 1928

Roy, P. G. (Ed.) *Old manors; old houses.* Proulx, Quebec, 1927

Traquair, Ramsay, *The Old Architecture of Quebec.* Macmillan, Toronto, 1947

Traquair, Ramsay, *The Old Silver of Quebec.* Macmillan, Toronto, 1940

Traquair, Ramsay (and others), McGill University Publications, *Art and Architecture,* Series XIII, Nos. 1-37

The Topographers

Godenrath, Percy F., Catalogue Raisonné of the Canada Steamship Lines. Collection at the Manoir Richelieu, Murray Bay, P.Q.

Kenney, J. F., Catalogue of the Public Archives. Ottawa, 1925

Locke, G. H., Catalogue of the John Ross Robertson Collection of the Toronto Public Libraries, Toronto, 1934

Piers, Harry, *Art in Nova Scotia.* Proc. N.S. Hist. Soc., 1914

The Pioneers

Arthur, E. R., *The Early Buildings of Ontario.* University of Toronto Press, Toronto, 1938

Arthur, E. R., *Small Houses of the Late 18th and Early 19th Centuries in Ontario.* University of Toronto Press, Toronto, 1940

Barbeau, Marius, *Cornelius Krieghoff, Pioneer Painter of North America.* Ryerson Press, Toronto, 1934

Barbeau, Marius, *Cornelius Krieghoff.* Ryerson Press, Toronto, 1948

Barbeau, Marius, *Henri Julien.* Ryerson Press, Toronto, 1941

Dyonnet, Edmond and Jones, Hugh. History of the Royal Canadian Academy. Typed MS in Toronto Public Library, written in 1934

Gagen, Robert F., Ontario Art Chronicle. Typed MS in the Art Gallery of Toronto, written about 1914

Kane, Paul, Catalogue of 1848 Toronto Exhibition. Scobie and Balfour, Toronto, 1848

Kane, Paul, *Wanderings of an Artist.* The Radisson Society, Toronto, 1925

Robson, A. H., *Paul Kane.* Ryerson Press, Toronto, 1937

Catalogue of first exhibition of Society of Artists and Amateurs of Toronto. The Patriot Press, Toronto, 1843

The Toronto Society of Arts. Catalogue, Toronto, 1847

The Impact of Impressionism

Buchanan, Donald W., *James Wilson Morrice.* Ryerson Press, Toronto, 1936

Buchanan, Donald W., *J. W. Morrice.* Ryerson Press, Toronto, 1947

COLGATE, WILLIAM, *C. W. Jefferys*. Ryerson Press, Toronto, 1943

HODGSON, J., R.A. Report on the Canadian Pictures at the Colonial and Indian Exhibition, London, 1886

LYMAN, JOHN, *Morrice*. Editions de l'Arbre, Montreal, 1945

MILLER, MURIEL, *Homer Watson*. Ryerson Press, Toronto, 1938

MINER, MURIEL MILLER, *G. A. Reid*. Ryerson Press, Toronto, 1946

PRICE, F. N., *Horatio Walker*. Carrier, Montreal, 1928

Art Museum of Toronto. Bound volume of catalogues etc, 1909-35. At Art Gallery of Toronto

Canadian Painters. Bound volume of trivia, 1880-1910. At Art Gallery of Toronto

La Société des Arts de Montréal. Catalogues, 1893-4

Yearbook of Canadian Art. Arts and Letters Club, Toronto, 1913

A National Idiom Emerges

BROOKER, BERTRAM (Ed.) *Yearbook of the Arts in Canada*. Macmillan, Toronto, 1929

BROOKER, BERTRAM (Ed.) *Yearbook of the Arts in Canada*. Macmillan, Toronto, 1936

BROWN, ERIC and JACOB, FRED, *Portfolio of Canadian Art*. Rous and Mann, Toronto, 1926

CARR, EMILY, *Klee Wyck*. Oxford University Press, Toronto, 1941

CARR, EMILY, Her paintings and Sketches. Oxford University Press, Toronto, 1945

CHAUVIN, JEAN, *Ateliers*. Carrier, Montreal, 1928

DAVIES, BLODWEN, *A Study of Tom Thomson*. Ryerson Press, Toronto, 1935

HOUSSER, F. B., *A Canadian Art Movement: The Story of the Group of Seven*. Macmillan, Toronto, 1926

HUNTER, E. R., *J. E. H. Macdonald*. Ryerson Press, Toronto, 1940

KONODY, P., *Art and War: pictures for the Canadian War Memorials*. Colour Ltd, London, 1919

MACDONALD, THOREAU, *The Group of Seven*. Ryerson Press, Toronto, 1944

ROBSON, A. H., *Clarence A. Gagnon*. Ryerson Press, Toronto, 1938

ROBSON, A. H., *A. Y. Jackson*. Ryerson Press, Toronto, 1938

ROBSON, A. H., *Tom Thomson*. Ryerson Press, Toronto, 1937

The Group of Seven. Catalogue of the 1922 Exhibition, Toronto, 1922

Quebec: A Fresh Approach

BARBEAU, MARIUS, *Painters of Quebec*. Ryerson Press, Toronto, 1946

DUMAS, PAUL, *Lyman*. Editions de l'Arbre, Montreal, 1944

ELIE, ROBERT, *Borduas*. Editions de l'Arbre, Montreal, 1943

GAGNON, MAURICE, *Pellan*. Editions de l'Arbre, Montreal, 1943

DE GRANDMONT, ELOI, *Cinquante Dessins d'Alfred Pellan*. Editions Parizeau, Montreal, 1945

DE TONNANCOUR, JACQUES, *Roberts*. Editions de l'Arbre, Montreal, 1944

Canadian Art in Brazil (Press Reviews). Rio de Janeiro, 1945

The Artists of the Second World War

SCHULL, JOSEPH, *The Far Distant Ships*, The King's Printer, Ottawa, 1950

SCLATER, WILLIAM, *Haida*. Oxford University Press, Toronto, 1947

STACEY, COL. C. P., *The Canadian Army Overseas*. The King's Printer, Ottawa, 1948

The Canadians in Britain, 1939-44. The King's Printer, Ottawa, 1945

From Pachino to Ortona. The King's Printer, Ottawa, 1946

Canada's Battle in Normandy. The King's Printer, Ottawa, 1946

Contemporary Painting

GAGNON, MAURICE, *Peinture Canadienne*. Pascal, Montreal, 1945

GAGNON, MAURICE, *Sur un état actuel de la peinture Canadienne*. Pascal, Montreal, 1945

HUNTER, E. R., *Thoreau MacDonald*. Ryerson Press, Toronto, 1942

The Allied Arts

BUCHANAN, DONALD W., *Design for Use in Canadian Products*. The National Gallery, Ottawa 1947

BUCHANAN, DONALD W., *Canadian Designs for Everyday Use*. The National Gallery, Ottawa, 1949

CARVER, H. S. M., *Houses for Canadians*. University of Toronto Press, Toronto, 1949

Canadian Image Number One. National Film Board. The King's Printer, Ottawa, 1945

Canadian Image Number Two. National Film Board. The King's Printer, Ottawa, 1948

The Arts in Canada and the Film. National Film Board. The King's Printer, Ottawa, 1944

PERIODICALS

Canadian Art, Ottawa
Canadian Review of Music and the Arts, Toronto
Journal of the Royal Architectural Institute of Canada, Toronto

The following periodicals, though not devoted exclusively to the visual arts, frequently carry articles on art:

Canadian Geographic Journal. Ottawa
Here and Now. Toronto, 1948-50
Queen's Quarterly. Kingston, Ontario
Saturday Night. Toronto
University of Toronto Quarterly, Toronto

FILMS AND FILMSTRIPS

The following is a select list of films and filmstrips produced on Canadian art. Except where otherwise specified, details as to rental or purchase may be obtained from the Canadian Film Institute, 172 Wellington Street, Ottawa.

Canadian Artists' Series (National Film Board)

Canadian Landscape. Two reels, colour, 1941. The work of A. Y. Jackson

West Wind. Two reels, colour, 1943. The work of Tom Thomson

Painters of Quebec. Two reels, colour, 1944. The work of Suzor-Côté, Gagnon, Fortin, Biéler, Lemieux, Masson and Pellan

Klee Wyck. Two reels, colour, 1947. The work of Emily Carr

Other Art Films

Eskimo Arts and Crafts. Two reels, colour, NFB, 1942

Holiday at School. Two reels, colour, NFB, 1946. The Banff Summer School of the University of Alberta

Living Gallery, The. Two reels, b & w, NFB, 1948. The work of the Art Gallery of Toronto

Loon's Necklace, The. One reel, colour, Crawley Films Ltd, 1949. Distributed by the Imperial Oil Co. of Canada. A west coast Indian legend told through the use of animated masks from the National Museum of Canada

Primitive Painters of Charlevoix. Two reels, colour, NFB, 1947. The work of the primitives of the Murray Bay district of Quebec

Third Dimension. Two reels, b & w, NFB, 1947. The work of contemporary Canadian sculptors

Totems. One reel, colour, NFB, 1944. The totems of the West Coast Indians

The work of Norman Maclaren and other animators is best seen in the following National Film Board productions: the "Chants Populaires" and "Let's All Sing Together" series; "Dollar Dance"; "La Poulette Grise"; "Chantons Noël"; "Fiddle-dee-dee"; "Begone Dull Care"

Creative Hands Series (Crawley Films Ltd., Ottawa)

A series of eight half-reel colour subjects in the field of child art, produced during 1949-50, it deals with the following subjects: model houses; paper sculpture; finger painting; design to music; weaving; picture making; paper masks; home-made music

Filmstrips

Better Design for Everyday Use, b & w, 40 frames, NFB, 1950

La Palme. Colour, 37 frames, NFB, 1950

INDEX

133

INDEX

INDEX

INDEX

136

INDEX

137

INDEX

INDEX

Printed and bound in Canada
Press of The Hunter Rose Co. Limited
Toronto, Ont.